*Transforming Disciples*

TRANSFORMATIONS
THE EPISCOPAL CHURCH IN THE 21ST CENTURY

# Transforming
# Disciples

LINDA L. GRENZ

CHURCH PUBLISHING
*an imprint of Church Publishing Incorporated, New York*

Library of Congress Cataloging-in-Publication Data
Grenz, Linda L., 1950–
    Transforming disciples / by Linda L. Grenz.
            p.            cm.
    ISBN 978-0-89869-598-4 (pbk.)
    1. Church renewal. 2. Episcopal Church—Forecasting.
    3. Discipling (Christianity) 4. Spiritual formation. I. Title.
    BV600.3.G74 2008
    283'.73090511—dc22
                                        2008014059

Cover design by Stefan Killen Design.
Study guide and interior design by Vicki K. Black.

*Printed in the United States of America.*

Church Publishing, Incorporated
445 Fifth Avenue
New York, New York 10016
www.churchpublishing.com

    5    4    3    2    1

# Contents

a note from the publisher

This series emerged as a partnership between the Office of Mission of the Episcopal Church and Church Publishing, as a contribution to the mission of the church in a new century. We would like to thank James Lemler, series editor, for bringing the initial idea to us and for facilitating the series. We also want to express our gratitude to the Office of Mission for two partnership grants: the first brought all the series authors together for two creative days of brainstorming and fellowship; and the second is helping to further publicize the books of the series to the clergy and lay people of the Episcopal Church.

# Series Preface

B e ye transformed" (KJV). "Be transformed by the renewing of your minds" (NRSV). "Fix your attention on God. You'll be changed from the inside out" (*The Message*). Thus St. Paul exhorted the earliest Christian community in his writing to the Romans two millennia ago. This exhortation was important for the early church and it is urgent for the Episcopal Church to heed as it enters the twenty-first century. Be transformed. Be changed from the inside out.

Perhaps no term fits the work and circumstances of the church in the twenty-first century better than "transformation." We are increasingly aware of the need for change as we become ever more mission-focused in the life of the church, both internationally and domestically. But society as a whole is rapidly moving in new directions, and mission cannot be embraced in an unexamined way, relying on old cultural and ecclesiastical stereotypes and assumptions.

This new series, *Transformations: The Episcopal Church in the 21st Century*, addresses these issues in realistic and hopeful ways. Each book focuses on one area within the Episcopal Church that is urgently in need of transformation in order for the church to be effective in the twenty-first century: vocation, evangelism, preaching, congregational life, getting to know the Bible, leadership, Christian formation, worship, and stewardship. Each volume explains why a changed vision is essential, gives robust theological and biblical foundations, offers guidelines to best practices and positive trends, describes the necessary tools for change, and imagines how transformation will look.

In this volume Linda Grenz, the founder and publisher of LeaderResources and a leader in the field of Christian education, addresses the topic of formation and discipleship in the Episcopal Church. The church of the twenty-first century will need to be a learning community, but formation in discipleship today too often entails simply a limited number of educational programs offered to child, teen, and adult "consumers" who move on if they do not find what they want. How can we make the transition from consumer religion to participatory faith in a time of stress and upheaval, developing models and spiritual practices to feed the growing hunger in our churches for spiritual growth, maturity, and vision?

Like Christians in the early church, today we live in a secular culture that can be apathetic and even hostile to Christianity. Living in a setting where people are not familiar with the message or narrative of Christian believing requires new responses and new kinds of mission for the Body of Christ. We believe this is a hopeful time for spiritual seekers and inquirers in the church. The gospel itself is fresh for this century. God's love is vibrant and real; God's mission can transform people's hopes and lives. Will we participate in the transformation? Will we be bearers and agents of transformation for others? Will we ourselves be transformed? This is the call and these are the urgent questions for the Episcopal Church in the twenty-first century.

But first, seek to be transformed. Fix your attention on God. You'll be changed from the inside out.

JAMES B. LEMLER, *series editor*

# chapter one

# Changing Church, Changing World

IT'S SUNDAY MORNING, 1952

Mom, Dad, and the kids arrive at church. Nancy is left with the teenaged babysitter in the nursery. Thomas joins the rest of the teenagers in the youth room downstairs, where their teacher will try to keep them interested in the Bible study lesson. The rest of the family settles into their usual pew. The priest, vested in a cassock, surplice, and stole, is assisted by a teenager who is both crucifer and server. The service is Morning Prayer and the prayers and lessons are in Elizabethan English. Bobby and Susan sit impatiently with their parents until the sermon, when it is time for them to leave for Sunday school. Susan goes to the third-grade class, where she hears a story about Noah and the ark and then colors a picture that she'll bring home with her. Bobby is off to the sixth-grade class, where he learns about the early Christians being thrown to the lions in Rome. He and his friends spend part of the hour pretending to be lions, silently roaring while the teacher's back is turned. Meanwhile, their parents kneel while the priest reads prayers and then they listen to his sermon before spending a few minutes at coffee hour chatting with friends. At the end of Sunday school, Mom and Dad gather the children and head home for lunch.

IT'S SUNDAY MORNING, 2010
Dad and the kids arrive at church in time for everyone to head to Sunday school. Dad brings Nancy to the Godly Play worship and she is greeted at the door by an adult, who invites her to find a rug square and join the circle of children with today's storyteller on the carpeted floor. Susan and Bobby are immersed in the story of Noah and the ark for the third week. Susan's group is in the music room, where they are learning a song about the animals in the ark. Bobby's group is in the theater, reenacting the story from the perspective of the animals. Afterward they engage in a lively discussion about what the animals might have experienced, their relationship with God, and how global warming might be a modern Noah story. The youth group, just back from a pilgrimage in Ireland, has been engaged in a ministry discernment process and Thomas has decided he feels called to serve as a eucharistic visitor. Today he plans to ask David, a man in his sixties, if he will serve as his ministry mentor. Meanwhile, Dad is in the parlor, where he leads a small group through a process of theological reflection on the gospel lesson of the day. A second group is discussing a chapter in a book they are studying, while a third group is watching a DVD down the hall. Comfortable sofas, the *New York Times,* and a smattering of resources about the environment are engaging another loosely assembled group of individuals in the library, who gather to read, drink coffee, and chat during this hour.

At the end of the hour, Bobby joins the procession as a torchbearer. The priest is wearing the chasuble that the youth group designed out of their pilgrimage experience; one of the deacons, vested in a matching dalmatic and carrying the gospel book, accompanies her. Susan sits with her dad in a circle of chairs around a central altar. Nearby there is a rug on the floor with soft toys for Nancy and the other little ones. Sometimes Susan helps entertain her sister and the other children, but usually she is engrossed in the service. Today Susan and her friends are leading the Prayers of the People, so she eagerly awaits her turn at the microphone and proudly reads her intercession while Nancy stands with some of her "rug friends," whom she has gathered to pray with Susan. The service uses contemporary language and is printed in a bulletin that also contains the hymns. Members of the congregation read the lessons and lead the prayers. At communion time, Dad, Susan, and Nancy all receive the Eucharist together; Thomas, as usual, is sitting with his youth group and receives the Eucharist with them.

After the service, Dad and the girls head to the lobby to wait for Mom, who is coming by to pick them up. Next weekend the children will be with her, so Dad checks the schedule to make sure that none of them are listed to do anything at church next Sunday. Mom arrives and the girls head off to Susan's soccer practice, catching lunch at a fast food place along the way. Thomas leaves with a promise to drop Bobby off at his trumpet lesson while Dad joins a group in the parlor to talk about what their church needs to do to help newcomers understand the Episcopal Church and its theology in the midst of the current crisis around the full inclusion of homosexual persons.

## a changing world

The church has always sought to follow Jesus' commandment to "make disciples of all nations" (Matt. 28:19) and to help Christians of all ages to grow in faith and the love of God. How the church makes and nurtures those disciples has changed over the centuries, in order to meet the needs of the people living in any given time. Yet those of us living at the beginning of the twenty-first century know the world has changed quite dramatically in the last fifty years: many people talk about a "paradigm shift" that is both fundamental and global. At the heart of this shift is the move from modernism to postmodernism and beyond, from the machine age to the technological age.

The machine became the primary icon of the Industrial Revolution. Machines not only dominated how people did work, they also came to dominate how people thought and organized their lives—and eventually even how the church formed its members in the faith. Machines led to the atomization of life. To invent a machine, you break down the work required to accomplish a task into a series of individual, discrete steps (atomization) and then create a machine that replicates each step. This process of atomization and the ordering of things into a linear, logical order, embodied in the scientific method, was applied to almost all aspects of human life.

In the realm of medicine, for example, instead of treating patients holistically, medical specialties were developed in which a doctor treated just one part of the body. Instead of a single person creating a product from start to finish, factories were designed in which a person added just one part to the product while it moved down a conveyor belt. Even decision-making became atomized and organized into bureaucratic organizations comprised of executives and committees whose primary reason for existing was to make a decision and then pass it along the conveyor belt to the next level.

The secular education system followed the same pattern. Instead of learning the principles and application of mathematics while mastering carpentry, for example, mathematics was divided into first-grade arithmetic, second-grade arithmetic, third-grade arithmetic, and so on. Children moved along the education conveyor belt, with each child receiving the same "dollop" of information at the same age, based on the assumption that we could break learning down into its smallest parts and administer it at the age-appropriate time when it would best be learned.

The invention of one machine in particular—the printing press—totally transformed education, making information relatively cheap and easy to disseminate. The education system became almost entirely print-based and dominated by information, and lost the earlier holistic approach that also focused on skills, values, and behaviors. Machine age thinking created an education "machine"— the school—that added a piece of information to the empty brains of students as they passed along the conveyor belt from one class to the next. Where in earlier times an educated person was someone who was prepared to provide leadership in society, now an educated person became merely someone who knew a lot of information.

The machine age gave way to the technological age, made possible and dominated by the computer and the Internet. Whereas the machine mechanized physical labor, computers mechanized mental labor, and in the process changed not just how mental work is done but also which ways of thinking are used and valued. The earlier machines made the process of *atomization* valuable; the computer finds its value in *connectivity*. The computer works by connecting seemingly unrelated bits of information and out of these creating order. Computer systems (networks) function organically, with information flows resembling turbulence patterns rather than linear patterns of order. The Internet is an organic system that embodies this nonlinear order.

While many of our systems are still organized by the rules of the machine age, they are gradually being affected by technology and incorporating new ways of being. A patient still goes from one specialist to another, for example, but technology allows each specialist to see a complete computerized record of the patient's medical history, allowing him or her to "connect the dots" between the information entered by ten other specialists. Computers have not only dramatically increased the speed of product development, they have also extended participation as well. It is now possible for people all over the world to work via the Internet on the development of a new product, without ever meeting each other face to face.

Education has likewise been dramatically changed by technology. Where the printing press created an information *expansion,* the computer created an information *explosion.* The problem today isn't getting information— it's finding what you need in the huge pile of information that threatens to overwhelm you. So education is becoming more a process of teaching students how to find, analyze, and use information rather than merely memorizing information. In the 1950s a child needed to learn the multiplication tables and how to use a slide rule. Today a child can use a computer to make calculations and doesn't even know what a slide rule is! Where students once consulted a multivolume encyclopaedia of articles written by experts in their fields, they can now consult a Wikipedia article written by anyone who chooses to. This paradigm shift is profound and quite disconcerting for people who grew up and spent most of their adult lives in the machine age. It can be difficult to understand how younger people think, organize themselves, understand God and the world. It can be hard to make the shift from newspapers to Internet news blogs, from trusting institutions and authority figures to assuming that they are automatically and universally untrustworthy, from visiting your neighbor next door to connecting on Facebook with friends you've never met. All of these shifts create a gap between older and younger adults. This paradigm shift is more than a generational gap—it is a profound change in the way we live and function as a society.

## a changing church

We see the influence of this paradigm shift in the church as well. In the past fifty years we have seen a profound change in the place of Christianity in the life of the nation. Formerly, Christianity and citizenship were so intertwined that most people saw no difference between the two. Now it is more likely that young adults will absorb the secular cultural norm that being a part of a faith community isn't important. While most young people have a spiritual life and belief system, it is not dependent on being a part of an organization. The Episcopal Church has made some attempts, but it has not yet found an effective way to engage young people beyond the age of sixteen.

While older adults tend to accept most of the beliefs and practices of their faith group, young adults are more likely to move easily from one faith group or religious experience to another, picking and choosing bits and pieces to fit into their own personalized spirituality and belief system. Jesus is not *the* way, truth, and life for them, but rather *a* way, truth, and life. In this "post-denominationalism" world people have much less loyalty to the denominations in which they were raised; they look for and participate in a congregation that meets their perceived needs, no matter what that church's denominational affiliation. People move from congregation to congregation and from denomination to denomination much more easily and frequently than in the past.

Another aspect of this paradigm shift in the church is that people today are much less ready to accept authority. There is a loss of trust in institutions of all kinds, including churches. Most young adults are not interested in the current controversies over ordaining homosexuals or blessing same-sex relationships, for example: they see these as merely institutional issues that simply do not reflect their social values or spiritual concerns, and they are not interested in participating in the church as an institution. While older adults may experience this lack of interest as a rejection of religion, they are missing the fact that these same young adults are idealists who care deeply about faith, spirituality, authenticity, a relationship with God, and serving others.

Just as secular education has been transformed by technology, so also Christian education is evolving to fit this new context. The ease with which people move between denominations means that Episcopal congregations tend to see people both coming and going more easily. Rather than offering a few sessions in the traditional once-a-year inquirers' class, the challenge in this highly mobile, changing society is, How do we form people as Christians in the Episcopal tradition? Furthermore, Christian formation in most Episcopal churches now occurs with much smaller numbers—and yet many congregations try to maintain the traditional classroom system with one (maybe two) age in each room. Instead of *educating* Christians, primarily children, by providing information to its members about the Bible and church traditions, the church increasingly is turning to *forming* Christians of all ages for ministry.

This change from education to formation reflects the same paradigm shift we have been considering. Early Christian formation that was largely based in the home changed to a model that fit the industrial world. Sunday schools, originally created to teach poor children to read and learn moral behavior as well as instruct them in the Scriptures, were eventually extended to the children of church members as well. While formation (instilling Christian attitudes, values, beliefs, and behaviors) still occurred in the home and community, the responsibility for education (learning information) was largely given over to the churches which, unlike parents, had access to a printed curriculum that provided a structured learning experience and made teaching content easy.

By the 1950s the church had almost universally adopted the secular education model of providing age-appropriate information in age-segregated classes. First and second graders learned Bible stories from the Old Testament: the creation of the world, Joseph and his coat of many colors, Noah and the ark, Moses in the bull-rushes, Abraham and Sarah—all were popular stories for younger children. Fifth and sixth graders often were introduced to the adventures of Paul and the early church, and young teens were taught largely moral lessons based on the parables and stories from the four gospels. The assumption was that children were best able to learn certain stories, concepts, and topics at certain ages, so, like the secular school system, the church divided its teaching into these age-appropriate segments and administered them to students as they passed down the hallway from one Sunday school classroom to the next.

Christian education of teenagers also changed as youth ministry developed as a separate form of ministry—usually apart from and not related to the youth education classes. Some youth would come to Sunday school, which focused on teaching information, while others only attended the separate youth group meeting for fun and inspiration. Youth ministers, often young adults, became members of church staffs valued for their ability to play the guitar and to entertain and inspire young people. Camps and conferences were added on the diocesan level, with programming tailored to the needs of youth, and the campus ministry movement expanded to meet the needs of college students.

Christian Education . . . follows predictable patterns. Progress can be measured. By contrast, how Christian formation takes place is harder to trace. Because formation depends heavily on the work of the Holy Spirit, it is not nearly as predictable.
— *Anthony B. Robinson*

On the whole, youth were thus kept outside the general life of the church while they grew up. In the Episcopal Church a common philosophy emerged saying that youth needed to leave the church for awhile (usually during high school and college) while they "found themselves." This philosophy supported the "separate but not equal" practice of isolating youth in groups for fun, fellowship, and "age-appropriate" experiences of the faith. It also led to the wholesale departure of young people from the Episcopal Church—most of whom never returned.

This model of education as "information transfer" worked reasonably well in the early 1950s—a world where the primary formation of disciples still occurred in the home, at school, and in the streets. Children growing up in those days learned what it meant to be a Christian simply by living in the community. They went to church weekly with their parents, who, along with other adults, modeled Christian behaviors, attitudes, and values. Public speakers at civic events used biblical stories to illustrate their points and named Christian values and beliefs. The American culture was steeped in Christianity and people were formed as Christians because they simply "caught" the values, attitudes, behaviors, and beliefs of the Christian faith from living in America. Therefore the church could focus its attention on informing its members about religion and the Bible with the assumption that its members would be formed as disciples of Christ with minimal, intentional effort by the congregation. Formation was a parental responsibility and a cultural reality.

## from education to formation

Yet a shift was coming. A study of soldiers returning from World War II revealed that the prior Christian education effort was not effective; men in the trenches often found they had no faith they could rely on. Adult education was usually limited to the "rector's forum," a lecture by clergy on a book of the Bible or a theological concept such as grace or forgiveness. The lecture might conclude with a little discussion, often in a question-and-answer format that demonstrated that the laity had questions and the clergy had answers. This "one-size-fits-all" event assumed that the primary need of adults was to acquire information about the Bible, the church, or theology—often the same information their priest had acquired at seminary. The standard joke about the rector recycling his seminary class notes was not so much funny as true.

In addition, Sunday school attendance declined while overall church membership rose. The result, as Bishop Whittemore of Western Michigan said, was that "we are not only accepting religious illiteracy for our children, we have at the present time no serious intention of doing anything about it."[1] Bishop Whittemore and Bishop Peabody of Central New York prepared a resolution that asked the church to prepare a standard "corpus of instructional material to be acquired by every child by the time of confirmation and by the time of leaving high school."[2] The churches' response to this resolution involved considerable debate among educators over the best educational approach for the new curriculum. There were those who, like the bishops, favored a content-based curriculum, but others favored a "relational" approach that taught students how to think theologically about the issues they encountered in daily life, using discussion and relationships as the primary teaching method. While the latter approach was adopted in the children's curriculum, the content-based approach was favored in the materials provided for adults.

After many years of research, the Seabury Series was developed and published by the Episcopal Church's Seabury Press. It was an in-depth, experiential Sunday school curriculum designed as an ambitious experiment, according to *Time* magazine. It was also one of the most innovative and forward-thinking curricula of the time. The series' creators recognized the need for in-depth education based on the premise of the *full* participation of all baptized Christians in the life and ministry of the church—from infants to the elderly. The series thus sought to go beyond merely informing children and youth about the Bible, God, and the faith, and instead to "form" them as practicing Christians.

In 1955 *Time* magazine did a full story on the series describing it in detail—a remarkable feat that demonstrated not just the uniqueness of the curriculum but also the centrality of the church in an age when a new Sunday school curriculum was considered newsworthy. "Instead of aiming to give children some Biblical and theological background for the faith they will later join," noted the article, "the program undertakes to make functioning Christians of them here and now."[3] The article goes on to describe the different stories and experience-based teachings offered in the curriculum. The parents of younger children, for example, were encouraged to use the questions raised in daily life as the basis for theological discussion: "When Mike discovers a sprouting potato in the kitchen, his mother explains to him: "A seed grows into a plant like the plant the seed comes from." "Yes, but why?" asked Mike. "That's the way the world is, Mike. It is God's world and God's world is dependable," said his mother." Games of "role-playing" were suggested for older children as a way of learning social and relational values: "At a summer resort a new girl walks down to the beach where a crowd is swimming. She doesn't know how to swim and stands watching from the shore. What do the others do about her? This leads to experience in drawing a new member into the group, and can open up talk of our obligations as Christians to share all that we have—our skills and good times as well as our money."

The developers and advocates of the Seabury Series caught the vision of baptismal ministry—they saw that a vital church was not dependent on its clergy but on a renewed and fully participating laity. They understood that *practicing* one's faith was as important, if not more important, than merely *knowing about* one's faith.

The Episcopal Church undertook a massive introduction program that included hundreds of weekend Parish-Life Conferences to prepare congregations for the new series. They dispatched mobile teams touring around the country to review study materials with clergy and laity and to train leaders over a nine-year period. Several thousand adults enrolled in the intensive two-week laboratory training program that was part of the curriculum process. The curriculum developers had "four necessary conditions" they urged congregations to have in place before they used the Seabury Series curriculum:

+ A group of individuals who were "genuinely concerned about the redemptive task of the parish"— that is, the life-changing impact of the gospel on the lives of people (what we would today call having a commitment to living out one's baptismal promises);

+ An emphasis on *family* worship;

+ A weekly class for parents and godparents (notice that other adults are not addressed);

+ Religious and educational preparation for teachers.

The last two conditions in particular led to the development of The Church's Teaching Series—a set of books for adults outlining the basic beliefs of the Episcopal Church in the areas of Scripture, church history, doctrine, worship, theology, and ethics. These books were intended for the laity but were not envisioned as classroom materials or curriculum for adults. In publishing this series the Episcopal Church became the only province in the Anglican Communion with a published collection of basic teaching about the church's beliefs.

Despite this massive training and promotional effort, however, only a third of the Episcopal churches used the curriculum; it ceased being published in 1967, and Seabury Press eventually was sold. Some felt that the curriculum was just too ambitious: it was too difficult for teachers to teach without a sustained investment in training, and it expected too much of students and parents. Others felt it put too much emphasis on "process" and relationships and not enough emphasis on content. It is likely that the series also fell victim to the societal changes of the time, as institutions began to lose their authority and people valued "grassroots" efforts more than a single national curriculum. Sadly, its demise contributed to the church's failure to fulfill the Seabury Series' primary goal of forming practicing Christians. The vision of a renewed church that excited and energized the developers and supporters of the series at the outset was dissipated by a host of distractions and decisions that gradually moved the church's attention elsewhere. It was also the last effort made by the Episcopal Church to produce an integrated, age-level curriculum for the whole church.

> Merely teaching content about faith, the reigning model of Christian education up until the last generation, isn't going to do the job. Rather, you will need to introduce people to the basic narrative of scripture, the spiritual disciplines of prayer and worship and the shape of Christian living. Formation will need to replace education as our model of Christian nurture. — *Jim Kitchens*

In subsequent years, curricula and education materials used by Episcopal congregations would be produced by a variety of organizations, such as the The Center for the Theology of Childhood (*Godly Play*), LeaderResources, dioceses (*Living the Good News*), and even parishes like St. Philip's, Durham, North Carolina, which developed the *Journey to Adulthood* youth ministry program, as well as traditional ecumenical publishers such as Morehouse Publishing, which partnered with Virginia Theological Seminary to produce *The Episcopal Children's Curriculum.* Some of these curricula retained the older model of education as information transferal, focusing on teaching students about God, the Bible, and the faith. But many incorporated aspects of formation used by the Seabury Series, providing learning experiences where participants were actively involved in ways that helped them acquire values, attitudes, beliefs, and behaviors as well as information.

It is clear from these materials that over the last fifty years the language used to describe the task of education has shifted to a focus on Christian *formation*. Christian educators began to use the term *formation* to emphasize the fact that all Christians need more than just information to grow in the faith. A holistic approach to Christian formation requires us to address all three aspects of human growth: cognitive (what we know), behavioral (what we are able to do), and affective (what we value and cherish). It is not enough to just know the Bible stories or the seasons and colors of the church year: Christians need to be full participants in the life of the church and able to fulfill their baptismal vows in all aspects of their daily lives.

## baptismal ministry

During the growth period of mainline churches after World War II, for many Episcopalians the church was a solid, comfortable, and traditional institution that reinforced their cultural values and societal behaviors and attitudes. The Sunday liturgy of Morning Prayer was almost entirely word-based, with an underlying premise of informing worshippers about God and the good life. The clergy were in charge and the laity received their inspiration on Sunday morning: their duty was to "pay and pray." Private infant baptisms were primarily social occasions, draining that rite of initiation of its power and influence.

Then things began to change. The ecumenical liturgical movement and the discovery of early Christian writings offering insights into the worship of the early church led to a renewed emphasis on formation and baptism. A "mini-reformation" of sorts began as the Episcopal Church and other denominations turned to a renewed vision of the church as the body of Christ that we become part of through baptism. Consequently, in most mainline churches the Eucharist was restored as the primary weekly worship service of the church and baptism became once again the church's foundational and communal rite of initiation that it had been in the early church.

"To be baptized is to be in Christ, to be members of his body, the Church," wrote the authors of the liturgical volume in the 1979 Church's Teaching Series, "and thus to share a common way of life.... It is a commitment to a life-style radically different from that of the world."[4] This vision of a renewed laity, fulfilling their baptismal vows and gathering weekly to celebrate and renew their life in Christ, stood in stark contrast to the theology and practice of the time. Seeing the Christian lifestyle as radically different from the prevailing culture was exciting and energizing for some and deeply disturbing for others.

The 1979 Book of Common Prayer emerged out of this context and contributed profoundly to a more holistic approach to Christian formation. The Baptismal Covenant, especially the five questions following the creedal affirmation, began to influence how Episcopalians understood their faith in prayer and action as persevering in resisting evil, as seeking and serving "Christ in all persons," and as striving "for justice and peace among all people" and respecting "the dignity of every human being" (BCP 304–305). The four contemporary-language Eucharistic Prayers offered in the revised prayer book provided a radically different theological understanding of God and humanity. Instead of "miserable offenders," people were presented as beloved children of God. Instead of seeing people as broken, sinful penitents in need of God's redemption, they became, as Eucharistic Prayer C phrases it, those "who have been redeemed by him, and made a new people by water and the Spirit" (BCP 371).

## THE CATECHUMENATE

As the church rediscovered how early Christians worshipped it also looked at how they were formed as Christians. The ancient process known as the catechumenate was revived as a way to bring new people into the faith and prepare adults for baptism.[5] The catechumenate is not a program with a curriculum—a "course of study" leading to specific a goal (in this case, baptism), but a process of formation leading to baptism. In the catechumenate a group of Christians commit themselves to walk beside an inquirer or catechumen, who begins by studying basic Christianity, decides to become a Christian, prepares for baptism, and then after baptism goes deeper into the meaning and experience of life in Christ. There are liturgical rites that mark stages in the journey and invite the whole congregation into the process. But the formation process is designed to respond to the questions, needs, and concerns of each individual catechumen rather than being a predetermined course of study administered in the same way to every seeker.

This process is often a fairly long journey with no predictable outcome. The initial stage is exploratory. When the participants are ready to commit to a time of further exploration, they are "enrolled" as catechumens during a Sunday morning service and the community begins a journey of prayer and practice with them that will take several months. A team of people share their faith, answer questions, and study with the catechumen, who gradually learns what it means to be a Christian both by hearing about the faith and by observing the church, participating in worship, and reflecting on Christian living. This time of study can take as long as it needs to, and will usually include formal study as well as informal conversation and participation in the life of the church. As in the ancient church, this process culminates in a glorious baptismal rite, often during the Easter Vigil service, and with much more drama than we normally associate with infant baptisms. Afterward, the catechumens continue in a time of *mystagogy*, in which they reflect on the meaning of their baptism and go deeper into the life of faith. The catechumenal process—with its public rites of passage, its engagement of many people, and the sharing in a dramatic baptismal liturgy—is a powerful and transformative experience for the congregation as well as the baptismal candidates.

When the church puts that much effort into helping someone become a Christian, it communicates to the candidate and the congregation that becoming a Christian will change you forever; it is the most important thing you can do in your life. When members of the church are actively involved in helping form a new Christian, it is a renewing experience that can be life-changing for them as well. Making new Christians is probably the most exciting thing a Christian can do—but most Christians never have that opportunity. The catechumenal process forms new Christians while it enlivens the faith of those who were baptized years ago. Congregations using the catechumenal process generally see a renewed laity emerge in their midst—people who are actively engaged in the baptismal life and ministry. The catechumenate's insistent encouragement to include children and youth in the full life of the congregation is also part of the vision of the church as the community of the baptized.

## finding a balance

The catechumenate and other process-approach curricula developed in the wake of the 1979 revision of the Book of

Common Prayer offered a wide range of materials and programs to help the baptized become full participants in baptismal ministry. Like many changes, the pendulum sometimes swung almost entirely to the other side—from "education only" to "formation only." Some programs were developed where groups would engage in activities, role plays, or longer simulations followed by discussions that were focused on how they felt about or reacted to the experience. In most cases they were helpful in moving people from thinking and talking *about* God and their faith to relating to God and internalizing their faith, but in some cases they opened up overwhelming emotional turmoil and encouraged people to be inappropriately self-revelatory in the quest for deeper self-understanding and a closer relationship with God, while not giving them the theological basis for understanding their experience, or adequate support to process their experience emotionally.

Formation is the participation in and practice of the Christian life of faith. It is the same process that nurtures (helps us to conform to Christ's way of life) and converts (helps us to be transformed from another way of life to Christ's way of life). Formation is the means by which a community's world-view and value system are transmitted.... Our faith (how we perceive life and our lives), our character (our identity and behavioral dispositions), and our consciousness (our awareness and predispositions to particular experiences) result from such processes.
— *Called to Teach and Learn*

In recent years there has been a move among Christian educators to restore a balance between education and formation. There is an increased emphasis on acquiring information, as educators recognize that particularly in a secular culture one cannot merely acquire the values, attitudes, behaviors, and beliefs of the Christian faith without understanding the primary biblical texts or the history, language, and theology of the church. A Christian education coordinator at a college-town church tells the story of meeting with her Sunday school teachers. They spent about fifteen minutes before they figured out the answer to one teacher's question: "Does Moses come before or after Jesus?" This story is a stark reminder of the need for the church to invest in finding ways to teach the biblical story and basics of the faith.

On the other hand, there also is an increasing need for formation. The world today has shifted from seeing science as knowing everything and solving all problems to seeing that scientific knowledge leads to uncertainty; we have moved from answers to questions, from a single worldview to multiplicity. The church likewise has moved from the center of society to its margins, as American culture has become more consciously multireligious rather than predominantly Christian. In this context, the church cannot count on either parents or the culture to educate or form children and youth as Christians. Many of the parents of today's children have been raised with little knowledge of the church, the basic biblical story, or even who Jesus is. Meanwhile, the culture has moved from actively supporting Christianity to being silent or even opposed to some aspects of faith formation. Public school teachers know they cannot talk about Jesus or name specific values, behaviors, or beliefs as Christian. Churches seeking to build or expand in a neighborhood sometimes find their neighbors opposing their plans. And a neighbor who dares to lecture a child about anything is more likely to get sued by the child's parents than thanked for their assistance in forming a child.

In a culture that is religiously diverse and increasingly secular, Christians are not likely to "catch" attitudes, values, beliefs, and behaviors that help them fulfill their Baptismal Covenant just by living in America. Many adult newcomers to the Episcopal Church grew up in other cultures and have been formed in other denominations or other faiths. Traditional church attendance is becoming sporadic even among committed Christians, making it difficult to engage people in a standard, linear curriculum that relies on regular, sustained participation. Family life is fragmented and often chaotic—making it difficult for the family to be a locus of Christian formation.

In addition to those challenges, the church today is, in some ways, faced with an entirely new task: how to form *adult* Christians. For centuries, most Christians have been baptized as infants, so the contemporary church has limited experience with forming adults. It has traditionally relied on inquirers' classes or newcomers' groups to incorporate adults into congregations. Generally led by the clergy, these groups would meet a few times and were largely designed to help Christians from other denominations understand the uniqueness of the Episcopal Church and make a decision about joining this denomination. Held once or twice a year, they tended to inform people about membership more than form them as Christians. The church needs to find new and meaningful ways to help people who have little or no Christian background learn what it means to become a Christian who lives out the Christian faith within the life and traditions of the Episcopal Church.

There also is an increased understanding of the need for *lifelong formation*—a commitment to acquiring Christian knowledge, skills, values, beliefs, attitudes, and behaviors throughout life. Given the diverse backgrounds of our members, newcomers, and seekers, the church of today needs a multifaceted process of making disciples. That process needs to assume that all of us have something to contribute to the learning process—and that all of us need to learn and grow in faith throughout our lives. God isn't finished with any of us yet!

The shift in the culture (which used to do some of our "formational" work but no longer does) and the shift in theology (to an emphasis on baptismal living) means that we can no longer get by with just content education for children, entertainment for youth, and the rector's forum for adults. That model assumes that the church has a supplemental role in helping Christians in their faith journey—and it only works in a predominantly Christian culture. In a culture that is increasingly secular *and* increasingly fundamentalist, the mainline churches no longer have the luxury of doing supplemental education and formation. The Christian community must be engaged in intensive, intentional Christian formation throughout the life of every Christian. And that formation can no longer be consigned to Sunday school—it must be integrated into all aspects of the congregation and the lives of individuals, families, and friends who share a commitment to "grow in the grace and knowledge of our Lord and Savior Jesus Christ" (2 Peter 2:18).

# chapter two

# Making Disciples

*Go therefore and make disciples of all nations, baptizing
them in the name of the Father and of the Son and of the
Holy Spirit, and teaching them to obey everything that I
have commanded you. And remember, I am with you
always, to the end of the age. (Matthew 28:19–20)*

The transformation of Christian discipleship in the
Episcopal Church is rooted in this scripture passage
from Matthew's gospel, which is often called "the great
commission" and represents Jesus' parting words to his
disciples. Transformation begins as an evangelizing process
which initiates a lifelong journey of growth in one's relationship with Christ, culminating in baptism. It continues
in baptismal living as part of the body of Christ, the presence of Christ in the world. The task before the Episcopal
Church is twofold: both preaching and teaching, evangelism and catechesis. "The Church is called to engage in
an evangelizing catechesis, which not only communicates
and nurtures the life of faith, but unceasingly confronts
and continually converts those within and without the
community of faith to gospel loyalty, convictions, and
commitments."[6] Out of this mandate have emerged key

theological perspectives that challenge how the church engages in its ministry of formation.

---

The restoration of the baptismal liturgy to Sunday morning and the focus on the Baptismal Covenant has probably done more than anything else to shape the Episcopal Church since 1979. While most of the attention focuses on the five questions after the creed, I want to begin at the beginning—with the renunciations and affirmations.

> Do you renounce Satan and all the spiritual forces of wickedness that rebel against God?

> Do you renounce the evil powers of this world which corrupt and destroy the creatures of God?

> Do you renounce all sinful desires that draw you from the love of God?

> Do you turn to Jesus Christ and accept him as your Savior?

> Do you put your whole trust in his grace and love?

> Do you promise to follow and obey him as your Lord?

The task of evangelizing catechesis is, first and foremost, to help people develop a relationship with Christ that empowers them to turn away from evil and sin and turn to Jesus. In the early church (and in some congregations today), candidates at baptism would literally turn one hundred eighty degrees—from facing west to facing east—signifying a totally new direction in their lives. This is, at the end of the day, the heart of what the church is about—accepting Christ as our Savior, putting our whole trust in him, and promising to follow and obey him.

We are called, not just to tell people *about* Jesus, but to help them form a personal relationship with him. We are called to form people as Christians—as people who are not just "believers" but people who are in relationship with God-in-Christ. The church is the body of Christ—the community of those who have been baptized into Christ's death and raised with him into new life. This is more than giving intellectual assent to a set of beliefs. It is even more than living a good Christian life, engaging in Christian practices, and contributing to Christian causes. It is a relationship and a commitment to "follow and obey."

One of the challenges we face today is finding ways to present "follow and obey" so that this message sounds like Good News to modern ears. We live in a time when many people want to lead or want to be independent—free from the influence of anyone or anything. And while that freedom is illusionary (we are all influenced by something and someone), it is a value many people hold dear. Add to that the need to "obey" and we are in real trouble! It is hard to find anyone who is looking for someone to "obey"—a word with largely negative connotations in our culture. So it is no wonder that we quickly slide through this part of the service before happily settling on those much more comfortable five questions after the creedal affirmations.

I think we need to reclaim and perhaps reframe these commitments. For example, "obey" is a word that comes from a combination of *ob,* "toward," and *oedire,* "to hear."[7] So "obey" might be understood in our age as hearing the Word and moving toward (following) where it is leading us. We need to see obedience itself as a process of formation, a process of being drawn into a deeper relationship with Christ and in the journey, being shaped more and more in his likeness.

Christian formation is a process of being sanctified, of being made holy. This is not something we do by ourselves—it is God's action. But it is in our turning away from all that separates us from God and in our turning toward Christ and choosing to walk in this path that we open ourselves to God's act of sanctification. We do not become Christians by learning *about* holiness; we are gradually formed and transformed into the holy people of God. That process begins before baptism, but God's inward and spiritual grace becomes visible and real when in the midst of the gathered community of Christians we renounce all that separates us from God, turn to Jesus as our Savior, and promise to follow and obey him.

Immediately after the renunciations, the entire Christian community recites the Apostles' Creed, which articulates the core beliefs of the Christian faith. Creeds are difficult for many people: they were written a long time ago and use language and images that are foreign in today's world. It is clear that most of us are not alone in our discomfort with at least some of the words or images in the creed.

There is an educational activity that has been done in churches and conferences that highlights this ambivalence. The leader asks the participants to listen as the creed is read slowly and stand up when they believe the words without reservations, sit when they don't believe, and hover in between if they are unsure. The end result is that there is much bobbing up and down as people visually signal their comfort or discomfort with different statements in the creed. The point to remember is that the creeds are the creeds of the *church*: as individuals each of us might not understand or totally believe this or that line. But the creed is the church's affirmation of its faith. There are times in our lives when we might not believe much at all—and others in the community believe on our behalf.

At other times, we are the ones who carry the church's beliefs for others.

When we stand to affirm our faith in the words of the creed, we stand as a community. When we are baptized, we are baptized into that community—into the body of Christ. We don't all have to have an unreserved faith and believe everything without doubts to be part of that community. In fact, the reason we are part of the community is that the Christian faith is communal. Our faith is worked out in community. We come to faith and understanding of the creeds, of Christ's life, death, and resurrection through our participation in the life of the Christian community.

In the catechumenal process, an adult baptismal candidate walks with a group of Christians who serve as his or her companions. This journey may take weeks or even months as the candidate asks questions, participates in the community's life, and learns what it means to be a Christian. Baptism for the catechumens generally occurs at the Easter Vigil. The journey then continues in a phase called *mystagogy*, which means the interpretation of mysteries. This is the time when new Christians are invited to "go deeper," to reflect on and learn from their experience of baptism. And, not surprisingly, this is the time when they explore the beliefs in the creeds at greater depth. The creed has a different meaning for you *after* baptism than before—and its meaning will shift as you continue on your faith journey.

baptismal affirmations

One of the most popular aspects of the 1979 Book of Common Prayer are the five questions after the creed. They capture in succinct, clear language the essence of baptismal living—of what it means to live as a Christian on a day-to-day basis. These questions also have been influential in shaping people's understanding of the church's ministry and the place of both clergy and laity. As individuals become aware of their vocation to proclaim the gospel, to seek and serve others, to strive for justice and peace, to continue in the church's teaching and prayer, then they stop looking for the clergy to do these things on their behalf and start doing them in their daily lives—and eventually they begin wondering why they can't do them in church. If I promise to proclaim the Good News, does that mean only "in the world"? What if I am called by God to exercise my baptismal ministry by proclaiming the Good News at the time of the sermon? Does the preacher *have* to be ordained? If so, why?

In more and more congregations, the lines between clergy and laity are being softened as laity begin to exercise their ministries. While it is clear that the majority of the ministry of the entire church needs to be exercised "in the world," it is also clear that all of God's people can have active ministries within the community as well. So these questions have helped laity become more aware of their ministries and have helped the church become more open to the ministries of the laity.

*Will you continue in the apostles' teaching and fellowship,*
*in the breaking of bread, and in the prayers?*
This first question assumes that everyone, both newly baptized and those affirming a baptism of many years ago, are engaged in learning and worship together. "Will you *continue*" implies that you have already been learning and worshiping in the Christian community. Being baptized is not the end to the journey; it is just one step along the way. The Christian is called to continue to learn, to participate in the life and worship of the Christian community.

Christian formation happens in community. Most of us "catch" the values, beliefs, attitudes, and practices of the

Christian life from those around us. We learn by listening, seeing, and doing. Before the apostles had any teaching to pass along to us, they spent years walking with Jesus and absorbing what he did and said. The Christian life today is no different. We learn from each other. And we learn by teaching. Unfortunately we learn negative behaviors just as easily as the positive ones, so it is important to reflect on our experience, to hold it up to tradition and the scriptures to see where we are aligned and where we are not aligned.

Continuing "in the breaking of bread, and in the prayers" highlights the role of worship in the Christian life. Christians are called to give thanks for all God has given us, to receive spiritual nourishment and intercede for others. The weekly celebration of Eucharist is the community's expression of being the body of Christ. In it we are renewed to go forth and carry out our ministries in our daily lives. We are nourished both by word and sacrament. And we bring our concerns for others to God in prayer. The liturgy is where our lives as Christians scattered is united with our lives as the Christian community gathered.

In our participation in liturgy, we are formed as Christians in many ways. Some are obvious: the scripture readings and sermon teach, inspire, and encourage us. Some are not so obvious: the hymns imprint images, phrases, and understandings of God on our hearts. (It is often said that people's theology is shaped by hymns more than anything else.) We are also formed in liturgy by very subtle things—the action of bowing when we approach the altar or an ambry with the Sacrament present embeds in us a sense of the holy and heightens our awareness of God's presence. The rhythm of the liturgical seasons mirrors the rhythm of our spiritual journey. The oil used to anoint us in a prayer for healing opens us to God's healing action in our lives.

Liturgy and fellowship are as important in forming Christians as the traditional learning experience. We need to find ways to be more intentional about engaging people in liturgy in ways that are formational. And we need to value the formational character of our liturgy and our "fellowship" as well as our teaching.

*Will you persevere in resisting evil, and, whenever you fall into sin, repent and return to the Lord?*

This question probably gets the least attention of all. We don't like to focus on our brokenness, so we give our assent to the question and move on. But there are great opportunities in this question for helping people think about and learn ways to resist evil. We begin by helping them identify what *is* "evil" and to become comfortable with talking about sin in non-defensive ways.

An example. When congregations try to begin a conversation about racism, identifying where it is infecting their lives as individuals and as a community, often those discussions quickly turn into a painful emotional experience that leads them to avoid the topic in the future. We need to learn how to talk about racism calmly. We need those among us who can model acknowledging racist actions without getting defensive or trying to justify or mitigate it. We need to recognize that racism is one of the evils of our time, that we are all infected with it and affected by it and that we all need to be working on resisting this evil. When we fail, we need to repent and turn to Christ to forgive, renew, and sustain us as we continue our struggle to resist this evil. There are many other examples—degradation of God's creation, violence, destructive anger, and so on—but racism is one evil that is shared by all of us. The churches in America could well provide a leadership role in our nation by being communities that intentionally work on resisting this evil, repenting when we fail and then getting up and working on it again.

*Will you proclaim by word and example the Good News of God in Christ?*
We tend to parse this question in such a way that "proclaim by word" becomes a clerical role (preaching and teaching) and "example" becomes a lay role (daily living). But the question doesn't do that—and gradually people are coming to realize that *all* of us are called to proclaim both by word *and* example. This does not mean we all have to take our turn at delivering sermons! But it does mean that we all need to find our voice—our way of articulating the Good News of God in Christ.

For some of us that means talking with our children or other family members at home. For others it may be speaking to a friend or co-worker. Still others are called to proclaim the Good News to strangers as they go about their day-to-day lives. Proclaiming the Good News does not need to be a sermon—or the street corner ravings of a religious fanatic. It simply means being aware of God's presence in a situation and being willing to offer God's word in a way that points others toward God. That might mean a simple comment, a thoughtful response to a question, or a willingness to share your faith story. Talking about God with others—*especially* outside the walls of the church—is a powerful formational experience. Learning how to express our faith, practicing ways of doing it, and gaining the confidence to do it in times and places where it isn't expected can strengthen our own faith as well as the faith of those who receive our words.

Proclaiming by example is much easier to envision. We are happy to ladle soup at the soup kitchen, help out at the church's yard sale, take sandwiches to the homeless sleeping under the bridge, or take up a collection to help the needy somewhere in the world. We understand that this is the word in action. And it is fine to "just do it." But often we blur the lines between being good citizens doing good works and proclaiming the Good News by example. I suspect that's why the question has "by word and example." If we are to proclaim the Good News, we need to *proclaim* it, not just hope that the recipients figure it out. We don't need to push religion or do all of those aggressive things that make us Episcopalians nervous. But we do need to learn how to share our faith, speak comfortably about God and Jesus, pray with others, and be open to or even initiate a conversation about religious matters.

*Will you seek and serve Christ in all persons, loving your neighbor as yourself?*

Serving others has been a practice of Christians from the very beginning. We often involve children and youth in service activities, with the understanding that this helps form them as Christians. Seeking Christ in those whom we serve and loving everyone isn't quite as easy or obvious as it might seem. We tend to think of ourselves as "bringing Christ" to the poor souls at the soup kitchen, rather than going there to encounter Christ who is already present in those whom we serve. Too often we focus on helping others in a way that merely reinforces our superiority. We have all these good things in life and these poor souls have so little—let us give them a little from our largesse. We then end up doing service as a subtle way of making ourselves feel better ("There but for the grace of God, go I").

This approach to serving others forms us, but isn't appropriate Christian formation! When we are able to shift from the charity model (I have, you don't, so I help you) to a compassion model (we are companions on the way), we can see Christ in the face of the other. It is in those moments that service is transformational. When we seek and serve Christ in those we meet, we encounter the risen Christ—and our acts of service become holy. If we seek Christ in our serving, we soon realize that serving others is a privilege because in doing so we are blessed by Christ's presence in them. Christian service forms us as humble servants of Christ.

"Loving your neighbor as yourself" makes this an even more challenging question. Loving our neighbor next door, a family member, social friends, and even co-workers is not a huge problem. But loving the stranger on the street who is acting decidedly strange, loving the person who is mean or even violent, loving someone who has done some great harm to you or loved ones is a much tougher proposition. Christ calls us to love our neighbor, to love the people we encounter in our lives—no matter who they are or what they've done. Love them as fellow children of God. This basic Christian practice of loving others is a foundation stone in Christian formation.

*Will you strive for justice and peace among all people, and respect the dignity of every human being?*
The last question highlights the Christian's call to work for justice, peace, and dignity for all God's children. We are called to go beyond alleviating the symptoms (hunger, homelessness, drug abuse) to addressing their root causes. While Christians are often good at passing resolutions calling for justice and praying for peace in the world, actively working for these things is another matter. Effective Christian formation equips us to look at the bigger picture, to see the patterns that create dire conse-quences for some people while protecting others. It needs to give us the courage to fight injustice, to right those wrongs even if it means we will lose some of our power, wealth, or position. Striving for justice and peace forms Christians by doing—everything from writing letters, crafting legislation, or speaking up in a meeting. Providing occasions for people to reflect on their experi-

ence and to recognize their call to strive for justice and
peace is an important part of forming Christians.

## the theology of baptism

One of the major changes initiated by the 1979 revision
of Book of Common Prayer was the restoration of the
ancient understanding of baptism as the definitive sacrament of full inclusion in the body of Christ. Because the
early church primarily baptized adults, men and women
were usually baptized and confirmed in the same cere-
mony. As the church grew and bishops were no longer
able to be in multiple churches on Easter Eve (the
preferred time for baptisms), priests began doing baptisms
and confirmation, which was an integral part of baptism.
The emphasis was on baptism and Eucharist and, in the
first four centuries, the church didn't use the term "confirmation" as a separate rite.

Confirmation in the early church was the laying on of
hands and an anointing that signified the receiving of the
gift of the Holy Spirit. The scriptural precursors to confirmation are seen in the book of Acts, in the story of the
Samaritan converts. After they had been baptized by
Philip the deacon, the apostles "sent Peter and John to
them. The two went down and prayed for them that they
might receive the Holy Spirit (for as yet the Spirit had not
come upon any of them; they had only been baptized in
the name of the Lord Jesus). Then Peter and John laid
their hands on them, and they received the Holy Spirit"
(8:14–17). Over time, the two signs of the imposition of
hands and the anointing with oil became the primary
actions of confirmation. The tradition of requiring a time
of special "age-appropriate" instruction for confirmation
did not develop until recently.

Prior to the 1979 Book of Common Prayer, Episcopalians were baptized in infancy and children did not receive communion until after their confirmation at about eleven to thirteen years of age. The revised Prayer Book, however, restored the ancient church's theological understanding of baptism as full initiation in the body of Christ, which meant children who had been baptized could receive the Eucharist at any age, without the requirement of confirmation. It also restored the act of chrismation at baptism. Previously the priest made the sign of the cross on the forehead of the child while saying the words "do sign *him* with the sign of the Cross in token that hereafter *he* shall not be ashamed to confess the faith of Christ crucified," but did not anoint the child with holy oil. Nor did the wording imply any conferring of the Holy Spirit. Today the priest anoints the baptized with oil consecrated by the bishop, saying: "You are sealed by the Holy Spirit in Baptism and marked as Christ's own forever." Thus it restores the ancient practice in which baptism and confirmation are part of a single rite.

I believe that in the coming decades, for the first time in our history, adult baptism will become normative in the Episcopal Church. We will still baptize infants, but with a rapidly increasing number of unbaptized adults in our communities, adult baptism must become a regular occurrence as well. This means we need to rethink the rite itself. The current practice assumes that the baptismal candidate is an infant, so we have tiny baptismal fonts where the priest can hold a baby over it and sprinkle water on the baby's head. These fonts work for babies, but think about an adult being baptized. He must bend his head over the font awkwardly while a few drizzles of water run down his neck and into his eyes. Embarrassing, uncomfortable, and perhaps even annoying—but hardly a powerful or mean-ingful symbol or experience. It is not unlike the seminary joke about needing a double measure of faith when receiving the Eucharistic bread in the form of a wafer: first you have to believe it is bread, and then you have to believe that it is the body of Christ. First you have to believe that this embarrassing ritual is a water bath that signifies a profound cleansing and even drowning to be raised to new life, and then you have to believe that the baptism is transformative!

If we want adults to seek baptism, we need to make that experience as powerful and meaningful as we possibly can. The baptismal action needs to be "writ large" and fit an adult. The churches that have retained the practice of full immersion have something to teach us: for them baptism is a powerful act that embodies the dying and rising to new life in Christ. While some Episcopal churches are installing immersion pools, this is likely to be a slow change in our architecture. But that doesn't have to stop us from working with adult baptismal candidates to explore ways of doing a baptism that helps that person truly experience being baptized instead of just "sprinkled." Some congregations have used temporary pools to do immersion baptisms. Others pour a whole pitcher of water over the candidate's head—which requires a larger vessel than most baptismal fonts. While this requires some logistical arrangements (such as providing a bath towel to dry off afterward), it is more likely to feel like something significant has happened than a few sprinkles on the head.

baptismal formation

Looking at Christian formation through the lens of baptism should have resulted in education that is different from the models of education practiced in secular society. Unfortunately, even the best efforts of Christian formation in the church are still largely based on secular education models of teaching content and fail to form Christians whose lifestyle is radically different from what it was before their baptism. The revision of the Book of Common Prayer, the expansion of ministry roles to include more people, and the move from education to formation were steps in that direction. But by and large, church is still a congregation and not a Christian community—that is, a gathering of people who *congregate* at a particular time and place to worship God and receive the benefits of his mercies and the church's ministries. They are congregations gathered around a minister instead of being ministering congregations. They are a people who are of consumers of religion instead of the people of God, empowered to be a powerful witness to Christ in the world.

In our society permeated by rampant consumerism, many Episcopalians approach the church the same way they approach any other place offering them something to "buy." Their attitude is: "I'm here to get what I want with as little cost to me as possible—if you don't serve me what I want I'll go elsewhere." This attitude is reflected in the tendency of people to avoid "joining" the church and making a pledge. They attend (when they feel like it) and put a dollar (literally one dollar) in the plate when they are there. This approach is unconsciously reinforced by faithful church members and clergy who are slowly "watering down" the faith and its demands in an attempt to make the church more attractive to newcomers. In our desperate need for new people, especially younger people, we have gone the road of lowering expectations. If we can just get them to come on Sunday and make them happy enough so they'll continue to come, we think we've succeeded.

But the end result is emptiness for both newcomers and the faithful attendees as well. If we want to move all of us from being consumers of religion to being full participants in the life of faith, we need to raise expectations and raise the vision of the promises of the faith. It costs more these days to be a Christian. I believe it is harder to be a Christian in an affluent, secular society than it is in a situation where life is a struggle. When you have nothing and don't know whether you will have enough to eat in order to live, it is easy to depend on God—you *have* to depend on God because you can't depend on anyone or anything else! When you have everything you need, it is hard to see how completely and utterly our lives depend on God.

Because our culture and circumstances do not naturally incline us to turn to God, we need to find a way to articulate the faith through real and powerful connections to daily life. Ironically, despite our occasional pessimism, the Episcopal Church is ideally suited to meet the needs of this current age. Young people, for example, are drawn to mystery, mysticism, and spirituality. Our liturgy fundamentally incorporates those elements and, with minor "tweaks," can easily and authentically respond to that need. Icons, candles, incense, chanting, silence are all things we can encourage that are already part of who we are. Young adults who are willing to spend hours in a yoga class or with a guru learning to meditate can participate in Taizé services, teach meditation methods for Christians, practice centering prayer, and follow the Prayer Book offices of daily prayer.

Young adults in general are turning to healthier ways to eat and are interested in growing the food we need using sustainable methods (vegetarianism is very popular among teenagers), and they have a real concern for the environment. We can broaden our traditional ways of talking about stewardship to include these concerns, encouraging the support of local food sources and helping people develop a respect for their bodies as part of God's creation. The church can foster an understanding that good stewardship means taking care of "our selves, our souls and bodies"; we can help people develop more balance in their lives, highlight the value of Sabbath time, and encourage practices that reduce or eliminate stress. We can build "green" churches and offer them as intentional "teaching churches" where others in the community can come to learn about how to incorporate different technologies into their buildings.

Worship is the primary classroom in which we have the opportunity to teach the faith ... to pass on the great traditions of the church. [This] means that we ought always to think pedagogically about what we are doing in worship. — *Jim Kitchens*

In order for Episcopalians to live into the "great commission," we need to go to where the people are instead of always expecting them to come to us. There are several successful models of people taking the Eucharist to the homeless and general public or engaging people in discussion and even worship services in a local restaurant or bar. The emerging church movement has reinvigorated the concept of house churches and expanded it to neighborhood churches that meet in schools or other public places. We need to take some risks and try different environments and different ways of taking the church to the people. We need to create multiple ways for people to become a part of the Christian community—through worship, learning experiences, service, prayer experiences, and more. In each case, we need to create intentional ways to invite people to move from their entry point into full participation in the life of the Christian community. We need to be intentional about building these Christian communities, even if it means giving up some of what we know as "church"—perhaps even our church buildings. At the same time, we need to find ways to use our buildings to serve the community at large instead of being solely an occasional sacred space for a handful of people.

These are only a few suggestions for how we can begin to move toward a participatory faith—a worship and congregational life that engages people fully, where people are "belonging, being, and serving." Instead of coming to church just to *get* something, people will come to church to *give* something (love, praise, witness, wisdom) and they will leave church with even more to give. People who are full participants in the Christian faith and life gather to give God praise and thanks, to love one another, to serve in Jesus' name—and in the process they are transformed by Christ, again and again, to be the people of God in the world God has created and the world in which they are called to be Christ-bearers.

Making this move means building relationships in the congregation that nourish people spiritually, relationships that empower them to risk living in Christ, relationships that encourage worshiping, learning about, and serving God and each other in new and enlivening ways. We must help people catch a vision so they will risk moving from a life in which they are just going through the motions to being fully *alive!* When new people walk into our churches, they need to feel the power of God's presence in a real and tangible way. They need to be enveloped by a sense of God's love and experience the profound joy of the Christian community.

Every congregation needs to find its own way, but the heart of the matter is that we need to raise our expectations for what it means to be a Christian. Today many of our congregations have a lovely worship service, nice programs, and friendly fellowship—but it is like music being played so quietly that you have to strain to hear it. We don't have to change what we do in radical ways, we just need to turn up the volume! Worship with more investment, risk opening ourselves to God's presence, actively engage in the spiritual practice of loving—even, and especially, those we find hard to love. Perhaps then, instead of finding us fighting about fine points of liturgy or about whom we ordain or about whether our leaders have passed the right resolutions or not, people would enter our churches, discover that we disagree radically with one another, and yet still be able to say, "See how they love God and one another. What an amazing place! This is none other than the house of God!" *That* would be a radical witness to the power of God's love to unite us in faith.

### baptismal teaching

The restoration of the baptismal liturgy to the principal feasts of the church and the main Sunday service has probably transformed the life of the church more than any other change in the 1979 Book of Common Prayer. What had become a largely private, family affair is once again a central liturgy in the life of the church. Reciting the Baptismal Covenant, and especially the five questions after the creedal affirmation, is changing our self-perception, giving worshipers a succinct summary of a vision for faithful Christian living. As congregations repeat the Baptismal Covenant over and over again, people begin to internalize these questions. On some level, they begin to ask themselves: How am I doing these things? How might I do them more fully, more faithfully? How can the church support me in doing them? How can we help our children and youth do these things *now*—not just when they "grow up"? How can we "live out" our Baptismal Covenant?

The Baptismal Covenant expanded on the previous shorthand vision of the faith "to work, pray and give for the spread of the kingdom." Gradually it dawned on people that just coming to church on Sunday mornings, putting a dollar in the plate, and "consuming religion" before going back to their "real life" was not enough.

People began to hunger for more—and the church developed a variety of ways to meet that hunger. Some of those ways became mere busyness, where people did more and more tasks with increasing burdens falling on smaller numbers of people as memberships declined. Other activities were personally fulfilling and served the congregation but didn't seem to transform either individuals or congregations. Yet others led people away from their congregations into small groups or occasional events that provided temporary fulfillment.

Despite some of the bumps in the road, the journey has undoubtedly engaged a broader range of people in the active life of the congregation. The church's liturgies generally involve a host of people in various leadership roles beyond the former "choir and clergy assisted by acolytes" model. Many congregations have moved from having committees that make decisions and raise or administer money to coordinating ministry teams that carry out the ministries. And a small but determined "Ministry in Daily Life" movement continues to nudge the church toward affirming and supporting the ministries its members carry out at home, at work, at school, and in their neighborhoods.

The Baptismal Covenant also became an important formation tool in revisioning how ministry was carried out by congregations, and the roles of clergy and laity in doing ministry. Instead of seeing a largely passive congregation gathered around a minister (who did the ministry), the vision became one of a ministering congregation—a vital congregation, actively *doing* ministry. Those congregations study and pray together to discern what ministries they were called to carry out as a congregation and who among them had specific gifts for ministry. These congregations take seriously the passage in Ephesians that in the church "some would be apostles, some prophets, some evangelists, some pastors and teachers, to equip the saints for the work of ministry, for building up the body of Christ" (4:11–12).

The movement to raise up lay ministry has more recently been called the "baptismal ministry" movement. This movement originally arose out of missional theology—the understanding that the people in a local context are best able to proclaim the gospel to their own people in their own language, rather than importing foreign languages and customs to communicate the gospel. When that missional theology met the spreading theology of the baptismal ministry of the laity, the concept of developing local ministry support teams was born. The congregation discerns and calls individuals to become preachers, stewardship leaders, priests, catechists, pastoral caregivers, and deacons to serve that congregation. Together those called to these roles along with others in the congregation form a ministry support team and covenant to an ongoing process of learning together. These teams become the primary pastoral leaders in their congregations. They sustain the congregation's life and support the congregation's members as they identify and exercise their ministries in the church and in the world. In other words, their role is "to equip the saints for the work of ministry, for building up the body of Christ."

The development of local ministry support teams solved a growing problem of how to staff small, rural churches, thus increasing their attractiveness in dioceses that were finding it difficult to fund full-time or even part-time positions in these churches. While the underlying theology is one that sees the whole people of God engaged in carrying out the ministry of the church, thus upholding the vision for baptismal ministry to be the model for the whole church, the reality is that money matters! If a congregation can afford to maintain the old "vicar of the village" model of ministry, it is likely to do so. Expanding that congregation's perception of themselves as a community of ministers in their village will require many more years of education about and formation in ministry.

"Do not be conformed to this world, but be transformed by the renewing of your minds," the apostle Paul urged the Christians in Rome (Rom. 12:2a). The Phillips translation says, "Don't let the world around you squeeze you into its own mold"—a picture that conveys more vividly what Paul meant. The world a person lives in has the power to form and shape us. It is like the wisdom parents like to give their children about choosing friends: "Choose wisely, because your friends make you who you are." When the American culture was more overtly Christian, it helped the church form Christians. Today the American culture contributes little to Christian formation and may in fact undermine the formation of Christian attitudes, values, beliefs, and behaviors.

As the diversity of faith groups in America rises, we have a greater need to be clear about who they are and who we are—what it means to be a Christian and an Episcopalian. When you live in a "Christian nation" you can go through life without encountering many people who challenge your practices or beliefs. But when more and more people are identifying themselves as having "no religious affiliation," or are active in other faith groups, Christians are more likely to find themselves responding to overt or implied questions. As children and youth learn about other faiths from their friends and ask questions, parents are struggling to understand, much less explain, the differences between faith groups. And as Christians fragment into smaller groups with distinctive theologies and practices, and fundamentalist Christians challenge the faith and beliefs of other Christians, Episcopalians have a growing need to understand and become articulate about their faith.

At the same time as there is an increased need for Christian education and formation, there seems to be less time available to do it. Individuals are working longer hours with fewer vacation days taken every year. Families are juggling more and more activities for both parents and children. Entertainment, education, and service activities compete with work and school for time and attention. Church often comes last on the list of things to do. The culture is a powerful force, forming all of us to be consumers. It leads us to believe that there is always something that can fix a problem, that give us happiness, that can make us feel better, look prettier, or do better. So, people today demand more and better programs, and are quick to criticize if something doesn't meet their expectations; they are slow to make a commitment, hesitant to pay much, and quick to leave if a church isn't meeting their needs.

It is easy for the church to adopt cultural values, attitudes, and practices without even realizing it is doing so. The church can get caught up in trying to do more and better programs in an attempt to meet the demands of consumerism. It can lower its expectations and adopt an attitude that says there are no demands of the gospel—just "God loves you and we love you" and that's about it. The church can adopt the cultural pessimism and enter a state of quiet depression. Or it can react to the culture with manic false optimism, ignoring the evils and brokenness that people know is present.

The good news is that the culture also has formed people who are hungry for community and relationships, for meaning, creativity, and spirituality. They want to make a difference. They are open to and eager for what the church has to offer. The church needs to help people understand and use the positive elements of the culture without being "sucked into" those elements that are detrimental to personal or family life—or do not support Christian living. We need to help people see that Christian living is about relationships—our relationship with God, each other, and ourselves; relationships that are in and through Christ. Congregations need to help people find meaning and live out their faith in ways that make a real difference.

If we fail to inspire and support people in their relationship with God in Christ, we risk having the Baptismal Covenant merely add yet more items to everyone's "To Do" list, which ultimately leads to burnout. If we burden people with things to do instead of helping them enter into a transformative relationship with Christ, they will end up being conformed to the culture instead of transformed by God. If we fail to form people as Christians—as the people of God living a radically different lifestyle—we will consign them to being formed by and conformed to the culture. The challenge the church faces today is providing a vision of another way of being and inviting people into a community that shapes and supports their life in Christ.

## reconciliation and wholeness

Today's world is becoming increasingly fragmented and complex. The shift from modernity to postmodernity affects every aspect of life, and the church has not been immune from this phenomenon. Many people are disoriented and upset by "relativism"—the postmodern tendency to value all perspectives without being willing to identify any one as superior to another. The postmodern stance is that while I myself may value a given practice or belief over others, I do not claim that it is inherently superior or universally the best practice or belief for everyone.

Many people today, especially young people, seek to understand and respect the perspectives, practices, and beliefs of others. This, obviously, is a difficult stance for someone accustomed to a theology that says that Jesus is *the* way, *the* truth, and *the* life. How can that be true if it is not true for everyone at all times and in all places? Postmodernity says that it can, in fact, be true for you (the Christian) and at the same time not be true for the Muslim, the Buddhist, or the atheist.

The shift from modernism to postmodernism contributes to the current fragmentation within denominations over differing beliefs and practices. Older adults, who grew up in the machine age and have lived their lives with modernism, struggle to find a comfortable place within this changing world. Younger adults, who have largely grown up in the technological, postmodern world, often don't see what the fuss is all about. They are far less invested in the current disagreements and more invested in listening, learning from others, and respectful dialogue than they are in arguing or coming to definitive conclusions. Ironically, they also are often attracted to ancient practices and a deeper commitment to Christ and Christian living than many of their elders.

All this is from God, who reconciled us to himself through Christ, and has given us the ministry of reconciliation; that is, in Christ God was reconciling the world to himself. *(2 Corinthians 5:18–19)*

In the midst of fragmentation, chaos, complexity, and conflict we are called to be reconciled and to be reconcilers. The mission of the church—that is, God's mission that the church, as the body of Christ, embodies—is "to restore all people to unity with God and each other in Christ" (BCP 855). That mission is rooted in relationships: we are called to be "at one" with God in Christ and to be "at one" with each other in Christ. Being "at one" with God and each other in Christ is both individual (my baptism, my baptismal ministry, my relationship with God) and communal (our congregation's mission, ministry, and relationship with God). A relational theology of reconciliation is both inherently Anglican and amazingly appropriate for the age in which we live. "God, who reconciled us to himself through Christ, . . . has given us the ministry of reconciliation" (2 Cor. 5:18). Our process of "making disciples" must help people be reconciled and become reconcilers in a world that is increasingly broken and alienated.

In the church we often speak of reconciliation and justice as if they were a single act. But the desire for reconciliation and peace almost inevitably collides with the desire for justice. The reality is that reconciliation is needed when there has been something that broke a relationship—and in that brokenness there is pain and real suffering. While forgiveness is an element in reconciliation, there is also a desire for justice. "Forgive and forget" is not enough; those who are injured deserve justice.

So how do we carry out the ministry of reconciliation? While Christianity offers the difference between retributive justice (which seeks to punish in proportion to the crime) and restorative justice (which focuses on the relationship and the need to make amends), the church also tends to focus on the "feel good" aspect of reconciliation and rarely teaches us how to ask for forgiveness or make amends. This may be one of the negative consequences of the 1979 Book of Common Prayer. In its legitimate move from the 1928 Prayer Book's theology of "miserable offenders" the 1979 Prayer Book minimized our sinfulness and the call for confession and contrition. The focus was on the goodness of the created order, especially all of God's children, and on celebrating the gift of Christ's life, death, and resurrection as salvation for all people. Yet it is possible that in making that shift, the 1979 Prayer Book has contributed to the modern tendency to avoid acknowledging and taking responsibility for one's participation in breaking relationships—a necessary prerequisite to reconciliation.

Christian formation today must help Christians learn how to be reconciled and to how to be reconcilers in an increasingly complex and fragmented world. This means creating environments in which people can be reconciled to God and each other in Christ—and helping people reflect on and understand that experience so they can be effective ministers of reconciliation. Creating such environments is more than just talking about reconciliation. It means challenging people to see the brokenness in their own lives and to see how we all participate in societal brokenness.

While people may be willing to acknowledge a broken relationship with God, with others in their lives, with themselves, or even with creation, they are often unwilling to recognize their participation in communal brokenness. Because we are part of the human community, all of us participate in the brokenness of the "isms" (racism, sexism, etc.), the actions of our nation when we kill others (even in "justified" wars), and in the degradation of God's creation. The fact that I may believe that I have not have done anything specific to contribute to societal brokenness does not allow me to escape from being a part of the brokenness. The "sins of the world" surround us and, like the air, we breathe them in and they become a part of who we are. If we are to be reconciled to God we need to first acknowledge our own brokenness, and then seek forgiveness and amendment of life.

Once most people come to accept the brokenness in their lives, is easier for them to seek forgiveness than it is to amend their lives. We often "talk a good line" in church. We talk about reconciliation, forgiveness, peace, and justice during the service and in our programs—but then we go home and continue life as usual. We forget that true reconciliation is transformative, that it radically changes how we live and move and have our being. If reconciliation is atonement (at-one-ment) then being restored to unity with God and each other in Christ makes a real difference in how we live our lives, do our jobs, and relate to our family, friends and neighbors.

The task of Christian formation is to help people understand that reality and to create environments in which transformation can occur. Reconciliation is a Christian formation task that takes honesty and investment in building relationships over the long haul. Reconciliation is not a "quick fix"; restorative justice requires more than just spending time with each other. How do we form Christians who are willing and able to pay the price needed to be a part of God's mission of making people whole again?

The theological imperative of the Baptismal Covenant has and will continue to affect the life of congregations and shape the way to "make disciples." When the vision of being a Christian was to attend church, pay one's pledge, help out occasionally, and be a good citizen, the process used to form people took one particular shape. Now the vision of Christian living is to be full participants in the congregation's life and ministry—*and* to do ministry in daily life, to proclaim the gospel in word and deed, to seek and serve Christ in all persons, to strive for justice and peace among all people, and to respect the dignity of every human being. Preparing, equipping, and supporting people in fulfilling that vision requires a much more extensive and intensive process than we have used in the past. If we are to "make disciples" who will fulfill this vision, we will need to continue to develop Christian formation programs and materials that are not just educational, but transformational.

# chapter three

# Building Blocks for Transformation

As we have seen, the schooling model of Christian education that informs people about the faith needs to be transformed into a model that *forms* people of all ages as faithful Christians. We can no longer assume that people learn the faith from their families or the culture, or that the church can "teach" them the facts in a few hours of classroom instruction a year. We need to move to a radically different way of forming Christians—a way that results in people living a radically different life, a life transformed by Christ. This chapter presents some of the ideas and practices—the building blocks—the church is putting in place as it moves in that direction.

## laying the foundation

### BUILDING RELATIONSHIPS

Building relationships is absolutely essential in making and transforming disciples. We live in a world that is increasingly fragmented, with families spread out across the country and with people moving and traveling frequently. In this environment, congregations need to be intentional about building relationships. Small groups, fellowship times, mentoring, and encouraging members of our congregations to spend time together are all ways to build relationships, especially small groups that are focused on doing a ministry or learning together. "See how they love one another" has always been the description of a Christian community. We experience God's love in our relationships with one another. If we merely focus on being effective at teaching people *about* God, we will deny them an experience *of* God. Relationships are thus important ways that we provide environments where people can experience God.

## A COMMITMENT TO LIFELONG LEARNING

One of the necessary building blocks for transforming the way we make disciples is a commitment to lifelong learning. And yet most congregations still communicate that learning is very important for children, somewhat important for youth (when they will come to church), and not very important for adults. Just look at your congregation's budget: "Where your treasure is, there will your heart be also." Most churches allocate a reasonable amount of funds for Sunday school and youth ministry but usually very little or even nothing at all for adult formation. What's more, most congregational leaders and clergy do not communicate that learning past the age of confirmation is normative. So, it is not surprising that about 80 percent of our youth disappear within eight months after confirmation and only about 10 percent of our adults participate in any ongoing formation experience.

Many congregations respond to rising demands on families by lowering expectations. We accept that sports are scheduled on Sunday mornings and that children and youth "need" to miss Sunday school in order to attend those events. We also have come simply to expect youth to disappear shortly after confirmation. In fact, we are almost proud of it—"Young people need to get away for a while and find their own way" we say to each other. "They all do it," we console a parent who is concerned about the struggle to get his or her children to come to church. Yet other faith groups don't have that expectation—and their youth do not disappear in their early teens. In fact, some groups, like the Mormons, expect that their young adults will give two *years* of their life to *full-time* ministry. They use that time to form young adults to be faithful Mormons and thus ensure that they will help grow the church by attending and inviting others to attend.

Our expectation is that our youth will leave—and they do. Moreover, we fail to create an expectation or environment for young adults to be a part of a faith formation process that engages them. We usually arrange the Sunday morning schedule so the children and youth are in their age groups while the adults are worshipping—and so almost guarantee that most of the adults will not want to or even be able to come for adult education before or after the service. If adult education is not at the same time as the children and youth programs, parents, in particular, can't attend. Who will care for their children while they are at adult education? If there isn't a program for the children and youth, the parents will leave for home as soon as the service is over. And if there isn't an expectation that adults need to learn, there isn't any incentive for the church to rearrange its schedule.

We fail to provide sufficiently challenging education and formation for our adults. If we expect adults to be transformed, we need to help them engage the Scriptures in a deep and profound way, rather than just using the Bible for meditative reflection, simplistic rules for living, or catchy phrases to use in speeches or arguments. We need to help adults, and youth learn how to study the Bible, rather than just reading their preferred translation and giving it their own interpretation. The goal should be that everyone should have at least a basic "first year of seminary level" education in the scriptures, theology, and church history.

Finally, we fail to provide faith formation for our older adults. In our anxiety about our lack of young adults, we often focus just on getting something going that will appeal to them. That is good and necessary. But we also have many older adults, some of whom have "been there, done that" several times. Most of them patiently go through whatever programs their church offers—again and again. We owe them programs that directly address where they are in their faith and/or in this stage of life. As we face an increasingly aging population that lives longer and longer, we need to think of ways to keep our most elderly elders engage in the learning process as well and not assume that once they are of a certain age they cannot or will not learn.

A commitment to lifelong learning takes time, money and effort—and teaching and communication from the clergy and congregation's leaders. We need to establish Christian education as normative—as something that all Christians do weekly for their entire lives. And the congregation's leaders need to model that by attending education events themselves. Clergy can mention a continuing education event in sermons and newsletters. Probably more important: they can join a group as a member, thus modeling that they haven't finished learning yet and that they can learn from a group led by a lay person. When people become vestry members, committee heads, and worship leaders, congregations can establish the expectation that those roles include attending at least one weekly adult education experience.

A simple guideline is for congregations to have at least one adult education experience a week for every twenty-five people in their average Sunday attendance. These don't all have to be "programs"—they can be built into ongoing events. For example, the choir could choose to add a half-hour before practice where they would study the scriptures of the next Sunday and how they relate to the anthems and hymns. The folks who serve meals at the soup kitchen could meet after the meal and do a book study together—and invite their guests to join them. Some groups might meet in neighborhoods: a play group for children of the same age with parents engaged in Christian education, for example. Other groups might be vocational (those working in medical professions meeting to study together) or location based (those who work in a region meeting before work or at lunchtime).

INVOLVING THE CONGREGATION

Churches also need to provide multiple offerings, and have ways to help people identify where they are on their spiritual journey, what they need, who else might share that need, and the resources that could help them meet that need. Some programs should be easy to enter (such as a forum with low participation expectations); others should require more vulnerability (a small group on a fairly "safe" or practical topic); and still others should be more challenging. Most of our congregations have a couple of people who dream up what they think others *should* want or have, and these programs usually end up attracting the same faithful few. It is better to have lots of smaller groups that are truly meeting the needs of the participants than to have just a couple of large education programs. The total number of participants and the true meeting of people's needs are more important than having a single "successful" program.

When I was a young priest I gathered the entire family-sized congregation for a fun afternoon of planning for the next year. We created a carnival atmosphere and had a great time brainstorming ideas and making decisions, using fun activities that engaged all ages. Included in that process was the question: "What should we offer for adult education?" The answer was: "Bible Study." We even identified what book of the Bible to study.

Knowing that people are more likely to participate when they have been involved in the decision-making, I therefore anticipated a reasonable response to the Bible study sessions. But the only ones who showed up were the same three or four people who always came to everything. Repeated announcements, personal invitations, time changes, and changes in the book of the Bible being studied did not improve the situation. When I stepped back and tried to figure out what had gone wrong, I realized that they had answered the question I had asked: namely, What did they think the church should offer? They thought a church *should* offer Bible study, and probably thought that others *should* attend it, even though they weren't interested in it and had no intention of attending.

The next year I asked different questions: "What do you need to be a more faithful Christian this year or to deepen your life in Christ? What are you willing to commit to doing serious study about?" We got a totally different answer. They wanted to learn about healing—and that ultimately led to the introduction of a healing ministry, the development of a cadre of lay pastoral caregivers, and a healing miracle that was transformative for many members of that congregation.

The question you ask largely determines the answer you get. The expectations you have largely determine the response you get. We need to raise expectations, not lower them. We need to ask more of those who are part of the

Christian community—more commitment to Christian values and Christian living; more dedication to a deeper spiritual life; more investment in the Christian practices of worship, service and community. We need to expect that every Christian will be engaged in lifelong learning on a regular, preferably weekly, basis. We need to ask people what they need and what they are prepared to commit to learning. Then we need to provide people with programs to meet those needs—and not expect them to attend the one or two programs we think they should have or like.

LEARNING COMMUNITIES

Being transformed by Christ requires a readiness on our part that includes both education and formation—experiences that help us understand who Christ is and create an expectation that the Spirit can and will act in our lives. We need to create and support programs, resources, and processes that help congregations become learning communities where people are transformed by Christ. The concept of "learning communities" is one of the important tools for shaping how we do Christian formation that is transformative. In a learning community, a group of people who share common values and beliefs are actively engaged in learning together from each other. A learning community also learns, as a community: the group itself acquires knowledge and skills that become a part of the group's life. Newcomers to the group then absorb that knowledge and those skills as they are integrated into the community. So a learning community operates on both the individual and corporate level.

The teaching function in a learning community marks a shift from the traditional model of a single authority figure who has knowledge and students who are there to receive and acquire knowledge. This "banking theory" of education in which the student is an empty "piggy bank" that the teacher "fills" with bits of information gives the teacher an enormous amount of power and authority, while it strips the student of power. In a learning community, the assumption is that everyone has something to contribute to the learning process and we all learn from each other. One or more group members may be the designated leaders of the group or a session, but these leaders are not seen as the sole owners of knowledge or truth. In some cases, they may be recognized as having specific knowledge or skills, but even in those situations, they are not given the same amount of power or authority as traditional "teachers." In many cases the leaders function largely as facilitators who help the group members discover, articulate, and share knowledge. The sources (usually plural) of knowledge are both external (from non-group members, often in written or audiovisual materials) and internal (from the participants). Group members are invited to share what they know from other contexts or from their own experience. Or the group may experience something together. In any case, group members then reflect upon and analyze both external and internal sources of knowledge to identify underlying principles, discern meaning, and integrate differing perspectives. Members of the group then come to a conclusion, deciding what they have learned. But the learning cycle is not complete until that learning is applied and the group sees whether their assumptions were correct.

Learning communities are generally characterized by:

* distributed control;

* commitment to the generation and sharing of new knowledge;

* flexible and negotiated learning activities;

* autonomous community members;

* high levels of dialogue, interaction, and collaboration;

• a shared goal, problem, or project that brings a common focus and incentive to work together.

Over time, learning communities tend to develop the following characteristics:

• capacity to adapt to local conditions and evolve over time;

• creativity and innovation;

• crossing of traditional disciplinary and conceptual boundaries;

• appreciation of diversity, multiple perspectives, and epistemic issues;

• community members who are responsible and skilled at diagnosing and addressing their learning needs.[8]

Some of the shortcomings of learning communities include short-term inefficiencies, a lack of central control, and especially a lack of predictability. Using the learning communities model requires an understanding of the strengths and weaknesses of the model and an ability to use them in ways that enhance learning in the church.

In a learning community, learning is not separated from action. Learning communities recognize that we are learning every day, in everything we do. The question is *what* are we learning and *how* we use what we learn. In a Christian community, the focus is on learning how to be more faithful disciples of Christ. Hearing about that from others, in sermons, lectures or reading books, tells us about ways to be a faithful disciple, but we don't really learn that until we put it into practice. Learning communities focus on helping people reflect on practices—on the way we behave as individuals and as a community. If we are to be Christ-bears—reconcilers who carry out Christ's ministry of reconciliation—then we need to act in ways that are reconciling. Just talking about it—learning all the scripture passages and theological terms, becoming proficient in dialoging about all of the various "issues" of the day—are all for naught if we can't empower Christians to act as Christians. The church as a learning community uses the "act—reflect—learn—apply" model to help Christians learn how to act as Christians.

---

## approaches to learning

### EXPERIENTIAL LEARNING

People learn best by doing. Learning is remembering and internalizing knowledge and/or skills so we can and will use that knowledge or skill later. But people remember only 10 percent of what they read, 20 percent of what they hear, 30 percent of what they see, 50 percent of what they see and hear together, and 70 percent of what they discuss with others—but they remember 80 percent of what they personally experience.[9] Perhaps even more interesting is the fact that people remember 95 percent of what they teach others.

Surprisingly, people who read books, come to church, hear sermons, and perhaps attend occasional adult forums actually learn and remember very little about the Bible or the Christian faith. Our children and youth programs with their focus on hands-on activities and projects are much better at incorporating experiential learning, while our adult programs still rely on the printed and spoken word—though the practice of adults breaking into small groups to study a topic or practice prayer are common examples of how this principle is experienced in congregations today. The experiential learning model says that learning is best facilitated by a process that begins with a concrete experience, then observes and analyzes that experience in a disciplined way, and then applies that analysis to other experiences (abstract conceptualization), followed by trying it out—in other words, applying what is learned to a real-life situation and observing what happens and the implications for the future.

> The worship, the teaching and learning, and the fellowship life of the church transforms us, week by week, and throughout a lifetime, from disciples to apostles. Disciples are followers—students—of a teacher. Apostles are those who are themselves sent out by the teacher to teach.... Too often the church has allowed people to stay at the listening, watching, and learning stage of things, and has not made the move to send them out to become teachers, actors, and ministers themselves. — *Anthony B. Robinson*

So, for example, adults will learn more about the Bible if they start with something in their own lives (a shared or common experience); then identify the behaviors, core values, attitudes, assumptions in that experience; look at the Bible for similar stories; analyze what that story said to the original hearers (study translations, language, culture, context); and then ask how that biblical story applies to our story. Based on that, participants then decide how they might use what they have learned in changing their attitudes, perspectives, values or behaviors. After they apply that learning in a real life situation, they then reflect on what happened and ask how it helped them to be more fully who God created them to be as faithful disciples of Christ.

Many fine Christian education programs incorporate the principles of experiential learning. What we often fail to recognize, however, is that learning occurs experientially even when we are unaware of it—and sometimes when we wish it didn't happen. For example:

* A congregation that regularly disintegrates into a shouting match over issues when people disagree

teaches its members (including children and youth) that being a Christian means treating each other with disrespect, refusing to listen to the views of others, and caring little for their needs.

✦ A congregation that primarily "takes care of its own" by offering worship, education, and pastoral care only for its members teaches people that being a Christian means relating to those like me—the people in my church, my club, my neighborhood.

✦ A congregation with an outreach ministry entirely focused on doing good things for poor people communicates that Christianity is about being charitable but not about doing justice.

✦ A congregation with worship that is only easy for "insiders" teaches its members that their worship needs are more important than anyone else's. It also teaches visitors that the church is not open to them unless they are willing to work hard at figuring out how to "fit in" and participate according to the rules of the existing congregation.

✦ A church building that is not accessible for those with disabilities teaches its members that the church is only for some people. It also teaches those who are not able to negotiate steps or hear the sermon that they aren't welcome or needed in the church—and perhaps even that God doesn't love them as much as God loves those who can easily participate fully.

What we do, or fail to do, when we act as a community of faith is an experiential learning experience for all of that congregation's members. One way to learn from that experience is to invite members to reflect and analyze a particular action or way of being: What does this action say to others? Imagine someone coming to your church from outer space, with no preconceived ideas about God or the church. What would they see and experience? What conclusions might they draw from that experience? If you can get outside your ingrained assumptions and perspectives, you might be surprised to discover what you have been teaching yourselves about God and the faith. If you do that, you will have an opportunity to decide whether these are the lessons you want to continue teaching.

RELATIONAL MINISTRY

People learn best in a relationship with other learners whom they trust and who are committed to the same goals as they are. This concept is most popular in youth ministry—"relational youth ministry" highlights the importance of adults being in relationship with youth, rather than just giving them information and entertaining them. Youth learn from a mentoring relationship—from actively practicing the Christian faith and reflecting on that practice with adults who have a deep faith and are able to share that with young people. The assumption of relational ministry is that teachers do not "teach" so much as live the Christian life and walk with others who learn by observing, asking questions, discussing, and participating in the Christian life.

Yet it is often true that too much of a good thing can be problematic. Relational youth ministry that focused so much on adult/youth one-on-one relationships found that in some places they lost the value of relationships within community. Even in groups with a single adult there are potential difficulties. While youth learn from adults, no single adult can embody the fullness of Christ. Beyond just relationships, humans need to belong. The community is where Christians belong—where they find a safe place to share the journey in life and faith. There is a growing recognition that relational ministry is at its best when it is integrated into community.

While it is usually not called "relational ministry," this concept underlies the popularity of small groups in adult education. Prior to the 1960s, the most popular form of adult education was the adult forum—a setting where the rector or guest speakers talked and the people listened. Since that time the trend has shifted to small groups incorporating both experiential learning and relational ministry—and focused on building community. People often learn as much from each other and from the shared reflection as they do from the materials or topic at hand. More importantly, they gain the confidence to explore new ideas, try new behaviors, and commit to a deeper relationship with God because they feel supported by a group of peers.

One of the limitations of the small group movement is that these groups can become "cliques" that exclude others or become a "safe" place for people who are unwilling to risk expanding their relationships within the larger community. Some programs are intentional about inviting new people, starting and ending small groups regularly, and implementing other ways to prevent small groups from becoming "closed." One ongoing challenge the church faces is how to help people feel that they belong to the larger community while still providing intimate, small group settings.

The growth of the lay ministry movement during this same time also incorporated the concept of relational ministry. Many clergy left seminary in the 1970s and 1980s with a vision of working in a partnership relationship with laity. Some clergy found that they learned as much from the laity as the laity learned from them. This model of mentoring people in ministry was one that helped the church move from the model of teaching as just talking to a more mutual learning model.

## MONTESSORI

A concept related to both experiential learning and relational ministry is that of educating the whole person. Children's education took the lead on this with the Montessori way of seeing children as learners and of creating environments that foster the fulfillment of their highest potential—spiritual, emotional, physical, and intellectual. This method taught adults how to respect individual differences, and to emphasize social interaction and the education of the whole personality rather than the teaching of a specific body of knowledge.

The development of Montessori education was part of the movement from the strictly linear approach to learning to a more complex, cyclical, and integrated approach. The industrial-age view of education as dispensing knowledge in age-appropriate "bites" fails to recognize that some first graders are already using "fourth grade" knowledge and skills, while others aren't ready for or interested in what the adults have decided is "first grade" knowledge. Postmoderism accentuates the complex, circular, and constantly changing nature of life, learning, and knowledge.

The concept of educating the whole person helps us move away from a "one-size-fits-all" model of teaching and learning. In the church *Catechesis of the Good Shepherd* and *Godly Play* are very popular programs that incorporate the principles of the Montessori method. This holistic approach to people and education has also influenced youth and adult programs.

## MULTIPLE INTELLIGENCES

Another important approach to learning is the theory of multiple intelligences, which was developed in 1983 by Dr. Howard Gardner, professor of education at Harvard University. It builds on the earlier theory of differing learning styles and suggests that the traditional notion of intelligence, based on I.Q. testing, is far too limited. Instead, Dr. Gardner originally proposed seven different intelligences to account for a broader range of human potential in children and adults, and later added an eighth. These intelligences are:

+ linguistic intelligence—"word smart";

+ logical-mathematical intelligence—"number/reasoning smart";

+ spatial intelligence—"picture smart";

+ bodily-kinesthetic intelligence—"body smart";

+ musical intelligence—"music smart";

+ interpersonal intelligence—"people smart";

+ intrapersonal intelligence—"self smart";

+ naturalist intelligence—"nature smart."

Other intelligences have been suggested or explored by Gardner and his colleagues, including spiritual, existential, and moral intelligence. Gardner originally excluded spiritual intelligence due to its failure to meet a number of his criteria. Existential intelligence (the capacity to raise and reflect on philosophical questions about life, death, and ultimate realities) meets most of the criteria with the exception of identifiable areas of the brain that specialize for this faculty. Moral capacities were excluded because they are normative rather than descriptive. However, these intelligences are of real interest to the church so it is important to watch for the evolving research in these areas.

Within the church, this theory is most popular in children's education. The very popular Workshop Rotation Model™ is based on this theory. Programs for youth and adult incorporate some awareness of multiple intelligences, but most of them are still largely geared to words. However, the concept of multiple intelligences is an important component of educating the whole person. When we focus on communicating the gospel primarily or even solely through words, we fail to communicate effectively with those who best receive and process information in other ways. If we are to be holistic in our approach, we need to consider all of the ways people learn and share our learning experiences to use as many of those ways as possible.

SPIRITUAL FORMATION

Another dimension of educating the whole person is an increased emphasis on spirituality and spiritual formation. This trend is due in large part to the age in which we live: while many people do not belong to a faith community, most still describe themselves as religious or spiritual. And a significant number of them engage in spiritual practices, both those who participate in religion and those who don't seem to be drawn to the spiritual life.

In churches this trend has been reflected in various ways. There is a renewed interest in ancient practices such as chanting, praying with icons or rosaries, and learning traditional ways to pray. Monasteries and convents are often booked months in advance. Labyrinths and pilgrimages are very popular. Churches, seminaries, and education conferences are now offering courses on prayer methods or the spiritual life. Sales of books on praying the daily offices have far exceeded expectations and sales of spiritual aids such as candles, icons, and rosaries also have been strong. All of these are indicators of a spiritual hunger and a desire to find ways to connect with God.

This trend provides the church with an opportunity to reach out to those who may not be attracted to the standard Sunday morning service but who may respond to a different worship experience. A number of churches have had a strong response to meditative services with Taizé music (monastic chants in a variety of languages), candles, and icons or to traditional Evensong or Compline. Walking the labyrinth is sometimes accompanied by a service of Evensong or other sung service. The common elements of all these experiences of worship are a meditative feel, silence, chanting or other simple music based on ancient tones, candles—all designed to facilitate entering into a deeper relationship with God in prayer.

## MULTICULTURAL AND GLOBAL EDUCATION

Multicultural education is one of the newer methods in secular education. It recognizes that most educational programs and processes are built on the experiences and norms of the dominant culture. It seeks to broaden educational experiences by identifying practices that are discriminatory or oppressive, by minimizing cultural dominance, and by incorporating multicultural learning methods. Multicultural education is grounded in ideals of social justice, education equity, and a commitment to facilitating educational experiences in which all participants reach their full potential as learners.

At this point, the church has only begun to touch the surface of multicultural education. We might include a Spanish-language song or learn about Christians in another part of the world, their customs, food, and a bit about their lives. Some programs and leaders seek to identify and eliminate language and practices that are discriminatory or oppressive. But on the whole, the church is only beginning to look at ways its educational processes can help its members become global Christians—ready and able to live and proclaim the gospel across cultural barriers.

Ironically, the church has traditionally provided educational experiences that were cross-cultural. Missionaries traveled to share the gospel, learned about other cultures, and shared what they learned with those at home. Today we still have missionaries but they are fewer and their impact on the American church is smaller. Missionaries have shifted from being those who bring the gospel to foreign lands to being partners with the local churches, often bringing expertise that is not available locally or supporting the local churches in their proclamation of the gospel.

Meanwhile, the companion diocese program has become a major way that dioceses and congregations connect with Anglicans around the world. Companion diocese relationships are built on the model of being partners in mission:

> Companion Diocese Relationships are disciplined ways, agreed upon and shared in by the partners, to know from first-hand experience what it means to live inter-dependently. They recognize that the responsibility for mission in any one place belongs to the church in that place, and that each part of the world-wide church also carries responsibility for mission in every other place.

That mission includes:

◆ mutual encouragement and prayer for one another;

◆ intensified knowledge of and concern for one another; and

◆ the exchange of resources, both spiritual and material.[10]

In recent days the church's adoption of the Millennium Development Goals (MDGs) provides another opportunity for congregations to expand their members' understanding of and participation in the mission of the church in the global community. The danger is that the church will, once again, choose to support mere charity—the easy task of raising money perhaps with a "feel good" trip to another country to see the plight of the people there. The call must be for money to fund these efforts, but the church must also provide an opportunity for members to become engaged in advocating for justice. If we want to "eradicate extreme hunger and poverty" we need to ask what creates that extreme hunger and poverty. Who benefits from maintaining a system in which some people have more than they could ever want or need while others have little or nothing? What would need to change in the world—and in our lives—to ensure that no one lived in extreme hunger and poverty?

Christian formation is about helping Christians ask these hard questions. If we are effective in forming Christians, these hard questions will lead people to a deeper encounter with God and a transformed life in Christ. In other words, Christian formation should change our lives in much more profound ways than just inspiring to give a few dollars to a worthy cause.

## the ministry of the baptized

### BAPTISMAL MINISTRY

When the Book of Common Prayer was revised in the 1970s it was part of a movement to strengthen the ministry of the laity. The emphasis on "total ministry"—the shared ministry of the laity and clergy—often involved increased participation in the liturgy. Lectors, eucharistic visitors, chalice bearers, intercessors, and worship leaders became the visible symbols of total ministry. Gradually the term "mutual ministry" emerged, as the concept of shared ministry was expanded to include ministries beyond the sanctuary. A parallel "ministry in daily life" movement held up vocations of the laity outside of the institutional church. Today, all of these concepts are merging into the term "baptismal ministry": how each baptized Christian (of all ages) represents, bears witness to, and participates in the reconciling work of Christ as well as taking "their place in the life, work and governance of the church" (BCP 855).

The focus on baptismal ministry has led to integrating Christian formation with systems transformation. What does church look like when everyone is called into and supported in exercising their ministry? How do we prepare and support people in doing ministry? In some dioceses, such as Northern Michigan, this has resulted in developing baptismal ministry support teams where people are called by their congregations to serve as preachers, priests, catechists, stewardship leaders, deacons, and so on. These teams learn together, are commissioned/ordained together, and are charged with the responsibility of supporting the ministries of the whole congregation.

In some congregations, baptismal ministry means expanding the vision of who is doing ministry. Educators in children's ministries, in particular, have highlighted the vision of children as ministers as well as recipients of ministry. Other congregations have applied the same concept to older adults and others who are traditionally seen as those who are "ministered to" rather than being valued for the ministry they do. Still other congregations and dioceses are focusing on a vision of baptismal ministry as extending beyond the institutional church to the arena of "ministry in daily life."

The focus on baptismal ministry leads to an emphasis on ministry discernment, equipping people for ministry and supporting them in ministry. Now the question is not: What do people need to learn about God, the Bible, the church, and the faith in order to be "good and faithful Christians"? Now the question is: What do people need to do the ministry God is calling them to do? This means that congregations need to provide their members with educational and formational experiences that enable them to sharpen or acquire skills, develop Christian values, attitudes, and perspectives, and be inspired to make significant commitments of time, talent, and treasure—as well as learning about God, the Bible, the church, and the faith.

## BAPTISMAL LIVING

A shift in language from baptismal *ministry* to baptismal *living* has emerged in the last couple of years. It is a shift designed to help the church refocus ministry not as something that happens in only church—generally on Sunday morning—but as something we live and do in the world. In the normal human desire to revert to that which is familiar and safe, the church domesticated the theology of baptism by focusing on including laity in various liturgical roles. While that is important—how we worship does shape who we are—it should also *reflect* who we are. In other words, the way we worship on Sundays should embody who we are the rest of the time. It is not a time apart, separate from the rest of life. Rather it is a time that reflects, inspires, nourishes, and empowers us for the rest of life.

> The Spirit is inviting us to re-envision how we bring people to faith under the more comprehensive rubric of Christian formation. Such a re-envisioning will broaden our imagination and deepen our practices of enculturating new Christians. We will begin to think of worship, small-group ministries and engagement in mission—as well as more traditional educational programs—as formative processes, shaping new and old converts alike so that they grow to reflect the life of Christ more clearly in their own lives. — *Jim Kitchens*

Baptismal theology emphasizes the promise of new life in Christ. Baptismal living is about living in that promise. What does it mean to be transformed by Christ? How do

I express that in my everyday choices, my relationships, my lifestyle? In the Baptismal Covenant we make a commitment to the ongoing practice of worship, formation, repentance, proclamation, service, and the search for justice and peace. These practices provide the framework for baptismal living—a framework that includes active participation in the life of the Christian community (formation, worship, repentance) and in the world (proclamation, service, peace and justice). Christian formation equips us for baptismal living and supports us in our life in Christ. The question for today's church is: How do we do that in a world that is increasingly secular, multicultural, and multifaith in nature?

## RE-VISIONING CHURCH

Christian formation is an essential building block of congregational life, but if we do not at the same time re-vision what it means to be church, our efforts at transforming Christian formation are likely to be undermined. The reality is that most of our church life systems are designed to maintain the church as an institution—to keep the round of worship services and activities of the church going. We have created a "church machine": we enter it at baptism, move through Sunday school and youth group, graduate to coffee hour host and committee member, and maybe eventually work our way up to eucharistic minister, vestry member, or senior warden until we finally come out the other end of the machine as "finished" Christian on our way to heaven. What is startling about this machine is that someone can spend a lifetime in it and still have a very minimal relationship with God, a minimal understanding of the Christian faith, and a minimal engagement in baptismal living.

We need to re-vision church to be a community of people who are transformed by Christ and are actively engaged in serving the world in Jesus' name. We need to re-vision who we are and how we are "the church"—not as an institution but as the people of God, as the community of those on a journey in faith. This is hard work because it requires us to let go of some of what we know and love. We cannot afford to waste time, energy, or resources on maintaining a religious institution for the sake of having that institution. That means looking at everything we do as a congregation and asking: Is this an absolutely essential part of being a Christian community that worships God and forms people for life in Christ? Or is it just a part of maintaining the institutional church? Would we be a Christian community if we stopped doing this, or did it another way? Transforming the way the church "makes disciples" has to happen in the context of asking ourselves these difficult questions and in looking at the whole system.

The emerging church movement is one place that might give the Episcopal Church some clues about how to go about doing this work. While there is no agreement on exactly what the emerging church movement is, the movement is having an impact on the traditional church— especially as it becomes clear that it is attracting young adults. In the United States the movement is led by evangelical Protestants, but the movement originated in the evangelical wing of the Anglican Church in England. And, ironically, those American evangelical Protestants are moving in directions that are quite compatible with the Episcopal Church—especially as they discover ancient traditions that have always been part of what we are.

Some of the key aspects of the emerging church movement are:

✦ They want to recover the sense of "being church" rather than "going to church" through intentional Christian communities of learning, service, prayer, spiritual growth, and worship—usually without buildings.

- They seek to "go out" to where the unchurched are, rather than "invite them in," where they are then formed to be like us.

- They intend to be indigenous expressions of the church, evolving in response to local culture where God's Spirit is already alive.

- They are grounded in the tradition even as they insist the church be relevant to today.

- They value praxis over theory, expecting to have their lives changed by the gospel as they purposefully engage in Christian living amid community.

- They want to recover a multi-sensory experience of worship and to develop worship forms that address the whole person and all our senses, rather than continue in conventional worship that is dull and unimaginative, and unworthy of the glory of God.[11]

---

sharing resources

GRASSROOTS RESOURCE DEVELOPMENT
This trend is somewhat unique to the Episcopal Church. Other denominations have, for the most part, maintained their denominational publishing houses or have worked out arrangements where there are a couple of curricula for each age group developed under the direction or in partnership with denominational staff. With the sale of Seabury Press, the Episcopal Church ceased to have that kind of "official" involvement in curriculum development and distribution. A study of education in the church concluded that our needs would be best served by supporting grassroots efforts. As a result, we have a number of small enterprises that produce resources or programs.

The advantage to this is that congregations and groups have lots of choices and we have been able to create more diverse resources that more quickly respond to needs and adapt to changing circumstances than the larger denominational publishing houses. Some of these groups produce resources that focus on a specific topic or area of interest and that allow congregations to tailor their learning to their particular needs and interests. Congregations and dioceses that have developed programs or resources to meet their needs have been able to produce and distribute those on their own or have a range of publishers to choose from—which opens up the publishing field to authors and programs that might otherwise never have been published. These grassroots programs tend to be easily transferable to another congregation, as they have been developed in a real congregation as opposed to a curriculum developed by a team of professional educators, some of whom may not have been in a congregation for years.

The disadvantage to this system is that we have no system of "checks and balances." Literally anyone can publish a curriculum, call it "Episcopal," and sell it to congregations. This means that the responsibility for checking programs and resources for appropriate theology, information, and educational processes largely falls on the local congregation. Congregations that have professional educators can usually screen out or adapt inappropriate resources. Congregations without a professional educator may use materials that they believe are solid and represent Episcopal theology but later discover that they have taught a generation of children, youth, and/or adults with materials that are Episcopal in name only.

A second disadvantage to the system of decentralized resource development is the duplication of efforts. Because these many enterprises are essentially competing with each other, there is no way to know if one has been investing a couple of years developing a program that essentially duplicates what is being developed by another. In a church where resources are limited, we cannot afford to duplicate efforts—or to waste time and money developing programs and resources that do not meet the needs of the people. The internet has been an invaluable help to many congregations in this regard, as resources that are currently available can be more easily identified online.

ELECTRONIC MEDIA AND THE INTERNET

Where and how we get our information has been dramatically changed by the internet. This is especially true for our children and youth, who have never lived without access to electronic resources. The computer has also changed how to develop and distribute resources of all kinds. It is now much easier for anyone to write and publish a curriculum—especially if it is distributed as an electronic file over the internet. Christian educators can easily adapt lessons to fit the local needs and share what they have created with others. Even sound and video files are easier to make and distribute than they were just a couple of years ago.

While the church cannot afford to compete with the slick video games, movies, and internet sites available to our children and youth in other areas, we can and do make use of these media. The Episcopal Media Center has served the church in providing multimedia resources, television ads, and radio programs since 1945. They recently introduced a variety of digital technologies that enable churches and dioceses to set up websites with multiple functions such as calendars, communications, video, audio, and so on.

LeaderResources, which I started in 1994, was a leader in the movement to develop and distribute curricula online. It now is an entirely virtual company with over fifty electronic curricula, plus e-books and print-on-demand books available online. LeaderResources also introduced the concept of "memberships," in which a congregation pays an annual fee based on its size and can then make as many copies of the program or, in the case of a multi-program membership, use as many of the programs as they need during the year. In the past couple of years denominational publishers have introduced increasingly sophisticated electronic curricula using this membership system—and have offered music and video CDs as well. These methods of developing and distributing resources have several benefits for the church:

♦ It is generally less expensive to develop and distribute electronic resources.

♦ Because the publishing house doesn't have inventory in the warehouse, it can easily fix mistakes and quickly revise curricula to keep it up-to-date.

♦ Some of the resources can be edited to suit local needs.

♦ Electronic publishing allows greater access to curricula development: individuals, congregations, dioceses, and groups who would never be asked to develop a program by a major publisher can "do their own thing" and either distribute it themselves or turn a successful program over to a publisher for distribution.

♦ Although we haven't seen many programs yet, electronic media does make publishing in different languages or for unique cultural groups possible. If those groups are willing to develop the materials, production and distribution is now cost effective.

While most electronic-based programs are still print/word focused, the church is developing video-based programming at a fairly sophisticated level of production.

As we do so, it is important to remember that since "the medium is the message," how we develop and distribute resources sends a message. We are a word-based faith tradition united by the Book of Common Prayer. What happens when electronic publishing makes it easy for every church to develop its own liturgy and its own lesson plans, handouts, images, music, and prayers? What happens when our worship is easily available to anyone on the internet? While we don't know the answers to these questions, it is important for us to reflect on how all of this is changing how we understand God and the ways in which the community forms people as disciples of Christ.

LANGUAGE RESOURCES

A significant aspect of coming to terms with ministry in a multicultural world is language. Thus one important building block in Christian formation and education in congregations today is finding ways to respond to the language needs of specific language groups. Hispanics, in particular, are one of the fastest growing populations in the United States, yet the Episcopal Church doesn't have many formation resources available in Spanish or other languages—and it is extremely costly to produce traditional resources in limited quantities.

One solution as to cost issues is to develop electronic resources, which allow individual churches to print as many copies as they need without having to print large quantities and store them until they are distributed. Another solution is to use resources developed by others, perhaps adapting or adding to them to include things important to Episcopalians. For example, the Roman Catholic Church has a number of good Spanish-language resources that are compatible with Episcopal theology. Instituto Fe y Vida has youth ministry resources, some of which are free (www.feyvida.org). Partnering with groups like this might allow the Episcopal Church to expand its language offerings by developing Episcopal versions of Roman Catholic resources.

The other issue is indigenous resource development. Dioceses and church leaders need to encourage and support local communities in developing resources that meet their own needs. Simply translating a resource or program developed in one cultural context into another language does not mean that resource or program will work or even be appropriate. Support means offering funds, structures (places to meet, an officially recognized "team," and so on), and resource people to assist in development, and then to actively promote the resource or program that is developed. Too often we say "develop your own resources" and then abandon the community and ignore what they produce. The church needs to walk alongside language and culture groups in developing what they need and honor what they develop. It is also likely that some of these resources could be used in predominately Anglo congregations to help them see the Christian life and faith from another perspective.

Recent developments in the Episcopal Church hold promise for the future. Theologians from five dioceses in Province IX and one from the Diocese of Atlanta are working to write basic materials that will form a comprehensive Spanish-language Christian education resource for Spanish-speaking congregations in the United States and in Province IX. The goal is to develop materials written in accessible, non-academic style that address the fundamentals of the faith, ministry, the scriptures, church history and governance, mission, Christian values, stewardship, and spirituality, with an emphasis on Anglican/Episcopal distinctiveness in these areas. This project is funded by the Episcopal Church and is led by theologians from the Hispanic community.[12]

## LEADERSHIP TRAINING

Before we turn to a survey of some of the programs and resources that are available to congregations today, we need to consider how these programs and resources will take shape in a congregation. Clearly, the church needs to invest in training leaders. Most congregations assume that with a little help any adult can teach Sunday school, lead a youth group, or facilitate an adult program. Because we assume that it is difficult to get anyone to volunteer in the first place, we are so relieved when they do that we hand them the program materials and then promptly abandon them. No wonder it is hard to recruit leaders!

If we are asking someone to teach a class or lead a small group discussion, most congregations have a reasonable number of people with at least some skills and background in how to do that. But formation processes that are *transformational* need different skills than teaching a class or leading a discussion. If we expect to move beyond the information and formation practices of the past, we will need to equip an entire generation of adult leaders with a new skill set to lead this work.

We have almost no way of helping busy adults in local congregations learn how to lead Christian formation in a way that is transformative. So people do the best they can by using their own school experience to teach a class. This usually results in education instead of formation, much less a transformative experience. Our church buildings (long halls with classrooms) reinforce the idea that learning content in a class is what is important, rather than reflecting on and practicing being a Christian. So we end up with yet another generation of Christians who know a little about the scriptures, God, and the church (gleaned from the few sessions they were able to attend) and little or no serious reflection on or engagement in a relationship with God and each other in Christ.

We need to develop a denominational system of training leaders, especially for adult faith formation. We have a system of training leaders for specific children and youth ministry programs (such as *Godly Play* or *Journey to Adulthood*, but almost no training for leaders of adults. Training for adults tends to be entirely focused on how to implement a particular program, rather than providing skills in how to invite and engage people in a transformational process. Clergy, for the most part, are still educated in the old "information transfer model" so they are generally ill-equipped to train leaders. It would be helpful for dioceses and regions to begin to develop groups of educators willing to provide this kind of training. Without it, we will be hoping for something that is difficult, if not impossible, for volunteer leaders to provide.

> The aim or goal of the Church's catechetical ministry is, with God's help, to become communities of persons who are devoted to assisting each other, and who are compelled to live fully the life of faith into which they have been baptized. — *Called to Teach and Learn*

If you ask people to lead an education and formation group, support them in their ministry. This means making sure they have the materials and supplies they need and providing them with someone who can answer questions or help out when they encounter problems. It also means running interference—almost every leader will have someone who complains about something. Leaders need someone who will intercept the most difficult complainers and negotiate a solution. Sometimes the leader needs to be given honest feedback. But often the complainer needs help in reframing the situation: just because you don't like how the leader is conducting the program or what he/she is saying, that doesn't mean the leader is wrong. Many groups in our congregations have a classic naysayer or two, and we tend to allow them to drain the energy of the entire group. Supporting leaders means having someone available who can help chronic complainers learn to focus on something good that they can affirm instead of focusing on their latest complaint. It also means establishing and maintaining a culture of affirmation rather than supporting a culture of criticism and complaint.

Remember to affirm and thank your leaders—of all ages. We tend to do this by making a quick announcement at the end of the school year. "And we thank all of our church school teachers for their hard work this year." We might even give them a token gift. Somehow I suspect that most of our teachers don't really find that very affirming. Find ways to affirm and thank your leaders throughout the year. Ask parents and participants to write a thank-you note at some point during the year when they notice something specific that the leader did that they appreciate. Even an email works, although a handwritten note probably has a greater impact. The clergy, wardens, and vestry leaders can do so as well—or simply to remember to say "thanks for your ministry" when they see the person. I am blessed to be in a congregation where the clergy and lay leaders regularly thank each other at the end of the service, and it is surprising how much that graciousness matters. Develop the practice of being gracious to one another—it is a Christian practice that will eventually spill over into the rest of your lives.

BEST PRAXIS

The church needs to identify the programs, processes, and people that use the best theory and praxis (practices) in doing Christian formation. Congregations then need to use them consistently and support those who develop, produce, and lead them.

What we tend to do is one of two things: 1) we use the program, processes, and people we know best; or 2) we look for the "magic bullet" that will quickly and easily "fix" whatever problem we have. The primary measure of success we use is attendance. So we look for familiar, popular programs that will attract the largest number of participants.

The problem with that strategy is that the familiar and popular may not be the best. They might, in fact, have unintended consequences that can even be detrimental. Our failure to evaluate what we do by any real means other than attendance means we may never know what impact a particular program, way of doing things, or leader has on the participants. The best measure of a good program, process, or leader is to look at the results. Are people's lives transformed by Christ? They may come to the sessions, love the leader, and rave about the program, but if it has no impact on their daily life as a disciple of Christ, it is not the best!

The church tends to invest in studying problems. We are far more likely to study why something *isn't* working than we are to study what *is* working. Those studies generally result in reports that gather dust sitting on a shelf somewhere. More importantly, an unintended consequence of these studies is that they encourage the growth of the problem! Whatever you focus on in a system grows. So, if you focus on problems, they tend to grow. If you focus on what works, however small it is, that small flame of good news will grow and spread. So, we need to invest in identifying what works—where in our congregations are people already learning about God in ways that are transformative? Who are the people who are already helping others deepen their relationship with Christ? What are we doing that is already helping people live more faithfully as disciples of Christ?

If you start with what works, you can build on that. If the adults involved in leading the youth ministry talk about how that experience has transformed their lives, recognize that the youth ministry program is, in fact, also an adult faith formation and leadership development process. Celebrate and invest in that. If the adults teaching Sunday school acknowledge that they are learning more about the Bible there than anywhere else—recognize that one of the best ways to engage adults in Bible study is for them to teach it! Celebrate and invest in that. If those who take communion to those unable to attend church find their faith grows in doing this ministry—recognize and support that as a means of faith formation. Celebrate and invest in that.

Talk with others about what programs, processes (ways of doing things), and people have been most helpful to them and their congregation. That doesn't mean it will work in your congregation, but it is worth looking at it. But don't just do what everyone else is doing—ask what results they see. Ask for specific examples. You want to hear stories about people who are living differently because of the program or process and not just enthusiasm about how interesting, fun, or easy it was. Granted, you can't always see results immediately, but if you ask people to tell stories, you will often hear whether a particular program or process primarily informs them about some aspect of the faith or actually forms them (shapes attitudes, beliefs, values, and practices) and creates a place where they were transformed (experienced conversion).

Once you have found something that works, use it consistently. Americans tend to like the quick fix. But faith formation is a process that takes a lifetime. And most programs and processes don't work overnight. Our tendency is to ditch a program the minute we encounter some obstacle instead of looking at the big picture and focusing on what is working well. If you have evidence that the program or process works, you need to stick with it and not be deterred by the first bump in the road or naysayer.

Support the people and organizations that develop programs and processes that work or leaders who are effective. The church often assumes that good programs will magically drop out of the sky or should be available at a low cost (because we are churches and don't have much money). But most of our best programs have been developed by faithful members of the church and are distributed by small organizations or by the individual or church where they originated—and they generally have very limited budgets. If we expect those people to continue to develop and distribute good programs, we need to support their ministry. Avoid the temptation to photocopy books or music or engage in any other illegal behavior just in order to save a few bucks. The dollars you save deny the developers funds they probably need as much as you do—and the illegal activity puts your congregation at considerable financial risk.

So we will now turn in the next chapter to a consideration of some of the best resources and programs that individuals, electronic and print publishing houses, and churches at the congregational, diocesan, and national levels have produced in recent years.

# chapter four

# A Resources
# Travel Guide

This chapter outlines some of the resources and programs that the church has developed as it has tried to respond to the cultural shifts of recent decades described in the first two chapters and to incoporate these shifts into its Christian formation ministry. The move to more hands-on, experiential learning is one way the church has responded to the challenges. The use of multimedia in Sunday school and the inclusion of children in worship are other attempts to bridge the gap.

While they are divided according to the age of the participants, some resources will apply to other age groups as well. In any case, it is always worth reflecting on what children are learning and how they are learning, because those children will soon be youth and their current learning experience will affect their needs and expectations as youth. Likewise, what youth are experiencing today will have an impact on what they need and expect as young adults. In addition, we often find that what works in one age group can be transferred to another age group.

*Godly Play* and *Catechesis of the Good Shepherd* are Montessori-based models of Christian formation, both of them rooted in the biblical story and liturgy of the church. *Catechesis of the Good Shepherd* was developed in Rome, Italy, by Sofia Cavalletti, a Roman Catholic lay woman. *Godly Play* is based on the principles in *Catechesis* and was developed by Jerome Berryman, a researcher and Episcopal priest.

In both programs, the children meet in a specially prepared classroom where objects are used to tell the story and provided for the children to use in play. A miniature altar and eucharistic vessels are used in the liturgy, while wooden animals and people are used in telling the biblical stories. Children then respond to the story in art, word, music, and action.

GODLY PLAY

*Godly Play* has a specific way of telling the biblical story and using the objects in play. Teachers need to learn and practice this method before they use it. The stories are told very simply, with simple props and without interpretation or moral instruction. After a story is presented, the story-teller and the children engage in a dialogue about aspects of the story that draw their interest. This dialogue is set in the context of wonder. The opening phrase "I wonder..." is used to engage the child in theological reflection. After a time of exploring the story, the children respond to it by creating whatever they choose—focusing on what they feel is most important, most interesting, or most puzzling in the story. This is "Godly play"—it is encountering God rather than teaching children about God as adults think we know God and/or what we think children *should* know about God. *Godly Play* knows that our faith stories are powerful and speak to our souls without elaboration, interpretation or explanation. It creates a sacred space where children can encounter and experience God.

Religion needs to be restored to its grounding in creativity, which includes both opening and closing tendencies, and results in the synthesis of playful orthodoxy rather than either dangerous extreme. The use of play, ritual, and narrative is the way to achieve such a synthesis. — *Jerome W. Berryman*

Jerome Berryman describes the educational theory and process he used in developing *Godly Play* in these words:

The educational theory of Godly Play is rooted in the pre-history of our species with respect to the use of ritual, story, and the creative process. Unfortunately, postmodern children are losing their ability to be active participants in narrative and ritual, which impairs their use of their own natural creativity *(imago dei)*. The use of Montessori's approach to education has been adapted to Godly Play in order to stimulate children's active participation in story and ritual and to awaken their creativity for the learning of the language, sacred stories, parables, liturgical action and silence of the Christian tradition.[13]

CATECHESIS OF THE GOOD SHEPHERD
*Catechesis of the Good Shepherd,* which preceded *Godly Play,* is the result of a long period of careful observation of children by Sofia Cavalletti and her Montessori collaborator, Gianna Gobbi, in Rome. Their website tells the story of its origins in the 1950s, when Sofia was asked to give religious instruction to a seven-year-old child.

She saw in that child, and in numerous other children since, a way of being in the presence of God that is both unique to the child and a gift to the adult who stops long enough to notice. Perhaps it is because Sofia went before the child with no preconceived ideas of what should happen that the child responded with such joy. Certainly her background in Scripture made it possible for her to talk about God in a way that opened and enthused the child as well as Sofia herself. From that day to the present time Sofia and Gianna remind us constantly to look to the child to watch for that sign of a deeply religious life—joy—and to always ask the question: "What face of God is the child telling us he or she needs to see?"[14]

Like *Godly Play*, *Catechesis of the Good Shepherd* understands that the adults learn from the child and their shared experience as the child learns from the adult. The adult is not present as a traditional "teacher" who has the knowledge and gives it to the child. The adult is present to establish an environment in which the child can learn, to observe, and to join the child in wonder, praise, and joy.

> If we want to help the child draw nearer to God, we should with patience and courage seek to go always closer to the vital nucleus of things. This requires study and prayer. The child will be our teacher if we know how to observe. — *Sofia Cavalletti*

The real advantage of both *Godly Play* and *Catechesis of the Good Shepherd* is that they work! Children learn core values and the stories that shape them for life at a very early age. Both programs engage children in a process that enables them to internalize the biblical story and Christian values, perspective, and behaviors. These programs are designed for and work best with young children—ages three through twelve (although some educators feel that this method loses its effectiveness at about the fourth or fifth grade, especially with boys who often need more "active" things to do). Berryman is now experimenting with using the method with elders in nursing homes—a logical idea given that we tend to become more "childlike" as we become older.

The primary disadvantage of both programs is the cost and commitment. Leaders are required to attend extensive and expensive training sessions and the cost of the objects is often prohibitive for congregations with limited resources. You can, however, make your own objects or find creative ways of addressing this concern. While both programs have firm guidelines on how to implement the program, *Godly Play* tends to be more flexible than *Catechesis of the Good Shepherd,* which requires teachers to be certified through a series of eight weekend trainings over a year. The training is excellent and teachers benefit greatly from attending. A similar training for certification in *Godly Play* is offered and strongly encouraged, but less intensive workshops are also available that prepare teachers without providing certification. Training is necessary to launch either of these programs: congregations cannot just buy the materials and expect to start these programs in the same way they might launch a new traditional Sunday school curriculum.

Both of these programs incorporate several of the current methods and tools. They seek to educate the whole child by engaging the child in worship, story, and play. They use experiential learning methods and utilize several of the multiple intelligences. And they help form children as full participants in the life of the church.

CHILDREN AT WORSHIP

Another trend that relates to the concept of educating the whole person is that of integrating children and youth into the primary worship services of the church. The Episcopal Church has long understood that "praying shapes believing," so participation in the liturgies of the

Book of Common Prayer is especially important for us. Our worship invites everyone into an experience that includes the whole people of God. Including children in worship has several additional benefits:

♦ It encourages leaders to "tell the story" instead of assuming that people know what the story is. Most adults under the age of fifty do not know the biblical stories of the faith or understand the basic theological or liturgical language of the church.

♦ It encourages leaders to attend to diversity. If you are looking at how to make your liturgy meaningful for children and youth, you are likely to think about how to make it meaningful to those who have never attended church, as well as to those from other denominations or faith groups, those from other cultures, and those with differing abilities.

♦ It encourages adult education. If children are in worship and have a Sunday school hour that is not during the time of worship, more adult faith formation options may be offered then as well. This supports the norm of "lifelong learning" instead of making learning something just for children and youth.

♦ It encourages a deepening of community life. Many adults are not accustomed to accommodating children in worship and find their natural behaviors distracting. Affirming the presence of children with careful teaching, discussion, reflection, and creativity can encourage members to grow in their understanding of what it means to be the body of Christ with distinctive and varying ages, gifts, and abilities.

The education of the whole person is especially addressed by Caroline Fairless in *Children at Worship: Congregations in Bloom,* an anecdotal teaching manual that tells the story of Fairless and her California church's journey to include children and youth in worship. Fairless went on to create an organization called Children At Worship, with consultants who will work with congregations individually or provide conference leadership and a website with an internet congregational membership that offers resources such ideas, prayers, dramatic readings, projects, book reviews, and art based on the scripture readings from the *Revised Common Lectionary*. Fairless and her colleagues have developed ways to help congregations prepare for and welcome children at their primary worship services.

Fairless invites us to take a moment and imagine what it would be like to have children fully incorporated into our worship services. "Imagine," she says, "creating an environment right there in your worship service, in which the children of God dare to respond to the awe and wonder and the mystery of God and God's gifts with a full range of expression, from joy and delight, to wordlessness and silence, from bodily stillness to expressive movement of rhythm and dance, from laughter to sorrow to tears and back to laughter again." When children are part of the worship of the church the entire congregation has the opportunity to write prayers and music, to tell the great stories of the Bible. "The energy is palpable; the excitement, celebratory;...the transformation unbelievable!" she concludes.[15]

MULTIPLE INTELLIGENCES:
WORKSHOP ROTATION MODEL™
The Workshop Rotation Model™ is built on the concept of multiple intelligences. It arranges several rooms with a focus on one of the "intelligences." Popular rooms include art, music, drama, puppets, story, kitchen, computer, movies, and games. You choose a Bible story or concept and develop activities for each of the rooms (usually four

to seven rooms, depending on your space and number of children). This means you are teaching the same Bible story or concept for four or five weeks, with the children rotating (in age groups) to a different workshop each week. The teachers, however, teach the same lesson week after week (with some age appropriate adjustments) to each incoming class.

The name "Workshop Rotation Model" was coined by Melissa Hansche and Neil MacQueen in 1990 at a Presbyterian church in Barrington, Illinois. They shared their experimentation with other churches and found others who had created similar ways of doing Christian education. "By 1995 enough churches in the Chicago area had successfully adopted the model to call it a movement," notes MacQueen. "Many of the original Chicago Rotation educators began organizing conferences. Several started publishing ministries." Over eight thousand churches in the United States and Canada have now adopted or adapted the model, and recently several major denominational and independent publishers have begun publishing Rotation-style curriculum.[16]

"We weren't trying to invent a new model—we were just trying to solve our problems," said Melissa Hansche, the Director of Christian Education at the Presbyterian church where the model got its start. What are some of these problems?

- bored kids and teachers;
- declining attendance;
- lack of Bible literacy;
- drab and uninviting classrooms;
- sedentary teaching;
- expensive curriculum (that's only half used);
- poor teacher preparation;
- trouble recruiting teachers.

Do these problems sound familiar? The decline in Sunday school is so widespread some see it as a sign of the times, spanning across all denominations. "Like a lot of other churches in our Presbytery, we knew we had to do something and soon," said Hansche. "And we knew that looking for yet another "new and improved" curriculum wasn't the answer either. Been there, done that."

The primary advantage of the Workshop Rotation Model™ is that children interact with the same Bible story or concept over and over again. This model rejects the popular lectionary-based concept with its weekly changing lesson because it sees repetition as something children like and need in order to develop a lasting memory and understanding of a story or concept. The Workshop Rotation Model™ also helps deal with the fact that many children no longer come to Sunday School every week—the story is repeated so those who are absent don't miss out entirely.

---

Instead of being a shotgun approach to Christian education where everything is covered and nothing is remembered, this is a bull's eye approach. The kids will remember the significant faith stories and have good memories. — *Linda Skaggs*

---

The multiple intelligences approach in this model "isn't a fad or merely kid-friendly," states MacQueen. "It is calculated to take advantage of our student's God-given thirst for multi-modal learning. Traditional designs have long attempted to teach through multimedia, but their frenetic lessons with six or more different steps, a game, a craft, Bible study and music all in 45 minutes left our teachers breathless. And few had the gifts to teach in each mode properly."

The Workshop Rotation Model™ has benefits for teachers as well because it provides an opportunity for teachers to get better at their lesson: "By the second week of the rotation, the teacher is already improving the original lesson plan for the next class. No more "if I only would have…" in the parking lot after class. No more Saturday night planning. No more recruitment hassles—teachers are happy to sign up for five-week rotations. And because the teacher is assigned to teach in the creative mode they are comfortable with, the teaching and learning experiences are enriched. No more lectures and music cassettes still in their cellophane wrappers, no more overused worksheets, or fumbling popsicle stick Jesus crafts." Only the grade-level shepherds (who don't have to do any preparation) sign on for the whole year. Other teachers can choose to just do one story, in one area. This means that people who otherwise would *never* teach Sunday school are willing to give five Sundays of teaching an art or kitchen project, especially if they are an artist or cook.

One of the disadvantages of this method is that it limits the number of Bible stories or concepts you can cover in a year because you spend four to seven weeks on each one. So what you gain in depth, you lose in breadth. Also, this method requires lots of creative effort as most of the materials cannot just be unpacked, read, and taught. The high level of interactivity means that teachers need to prepare projects. The counterbalance to that is that the rooms remain stable so you don't have to redecorate every time a different theme comes along. The art room collects more creative supplies and the theater stage collects more props over time, making the collection of supplies easier as time goes on.

The Workshop Rotation Model™ is highly adaptable to different circumstances. Small churches with limited space or few children can adapt the process by having a single room (or two) and changing the focus Sunday by Sunday. A simple banner or sign can announce that this week the room is "art" or "drama." If your age span is substantial, you will have to adapt some of the projects to make them age appropriate. You can also customize the decor and activities to fit different cultural or racial-ethnic groups, the location (such as rural or urban). and the amount of time, money, and effort you can invest (simple or complex).

While the Episcopal Church has a limited number of resources or programs available for families, several resources have recently become available that support families in seeking to baptize and become actively engaged in forming their children as Christians. As families have become busier and children are less regular at attending Sunday school, the need for home-based resources has increased, along with a need for congregations to engage and encourage parents, godparents, extended family members, and friends to become involved in forming children. "It takes a village to raise a child" is a common expression—and in an increasingly secular world where children have, at best, a couple of hours a week in church, it takes much more than just a church service and Sunday school class to form children. We *must* find multiple ways to engage the "village" in forming children. Resources like these allow congregations to support families and form villages to surround our children.

*The Seed of God/La Semilla de Dio* presents the essence of the gospel message to young children in a simple, but powerful way. Written in simple, clear language by Genelda Woggon and translated into Spanish by Maria Ludlow, the series presents the gospel message in five thematic books that fit a small child's hand.[17] This set of books can be a baptism gift from parents, grandparents, or godparents—especially the volume titled *Your Baptism/Tu Bautismo.* The full set of five books can be used to supplement preparation for baptism, especially in small parishes where there may not be a formal class but the parish priest does the preparation. The five books are:

1. *The Seed/La Semilla* tells of the power of God in the child's life.

2. *The Good Shepherd/El Buen Pastor* relates the parables about Christ's everpresent, loving care for his sheep.

3. *Jesus is Risen!/Jesus Ha Resucitado!* offers sacred history for little ears.

4. *Your Baptism/Tu Bautismo* explains to children and parents the signs of this sacramental moment that is entry into the Christian community.

5. *Living in the Light/Viviendo en la Luz* gives the call to deepen the baptismal life and walk faithfully as a child of the Light.

*Godparenting: Nurturing the Next Generation* (Morehouse Publishing) explores the history and theology of godparenting and offers plenty of helpful tips on how to be a faithful godparent. Being a godparent (or a parent presenting your child for baptism) is a sacred responsibility. This book is a handy guide as well as a keepsake gift for godparents, family members, and friends. Clergy and catechists preparing families for baptism can also use this book as a way for parents to develop an understanding of the role of godparents and the need for them to build a village to help them form their child as a Christian.

CandlePress (www.candlepress.com) publishes a number of small, inexpensive resources that help congregations support families. This includes books for children about baptism and Eucharist, books for parents and godparents, seasonal resources and *To Go,* a series of family resources that a congregation can mail or email to families to help them explore faith themes at home.

WHAT'S NEXT?

One important component that has not yet been adequately addressed within the Episcopal Church is the need for family education. The church must find ways to engage the entire family and provide ways for families to learn together—perhaps with other neighboring families. If parents don't know the basic Bible stories, they will learn them if they are engaged in teaching them to their children. The Bible stories themselves are the easiest teaching we have, and we can develop materials that give parents very short, easy things to do with their children. Other family resources might include graces for meals, a theme to talk about each week (with ideas for what to say or do), and activities that can be done in the car enroute to the next event. For example, *Live It!* is a resource (available from LeaderResources) that was developed by Margaret Hutton and Ann Willott for St. John's Episcopal Church in Jackson, Wyoming. It provides a simple card-sign for the kitchen table that families can use to reflect on a theme word and a scripture passage; it also provides an activity and a prayer. Families at St. John's have found that taking a few minutes during a meal, at least a couple of times a week, can bring church "home" and can engage parents in nurturing their children's faith.

The church also needs to establish parenting groups. Parents need help in how to be faithful Christian parents. We assume that they know what that means and where they can get the resources they need, but this isn't usually the case. The church sometimes needs to help parents with practical skills like discipline, nutrition, and achieving balance in family life rather than trying to do it all, in addition to those things that are specific to the faith: how to pray with your child, how to do a laying on of hands when your child is ill, why reading Bible stories to your child is important, how to help your child learn right from wrong, and so on.

Congregations need more help in how to identify, affirm, respect, and support the ministries of their children. Stories about children who carry out or organize significant outreach ministries occasionally are reported in the secular news, but these stories should be common in our churches. Children are called by God to live out their baptismal vows *now*, not just when they grow up but *as children,* and with a little help they can envision ministries that are significant and meaningful. They can be full participants in worship and can be powerful witnesses to God's presence in their lives. Their openness often leads them to articulate theological understandings and ask piercing questions. Adults in our congregations need to learn how to listen and learn from our children.

Congregations need to re-vision the liturgy to fit how they, as a whole community, worship and praise God in Jesus' name in ways that incorporate children. Liturgies need to be more open, more participatory, more powerful and, at the same time, simpler. They need to find ways to translate the faith into images—much as the church did with stained glass windows in earlier eras. Children, youth, and adults today learn from images and we need to pay more attention to the images on our websites, in our worship places, hallways, bulletins, and resources.

Churches need to find ways to proclaim the Word that is powerful instead of boring, and join in music that engages all ages. This does *not* mean guitars and drums in every service—a mode that appeals more to Baby Boomers than young adults or children! Some of the ancient, short chants can be very easy for children to learn and if used regularly provide everyone with memorized musical pieces that sustain us when no printed words are around. Since music is the primary way people learn theology (more than the sermon or classes), finding music that is memorable, easy to sing, and enhances a spiritual connection with God is one way to make our liturgy more accessible to children.

Finally, the church needs to find ways to engage the entire congregation in forming children. It takes a village to raise a child—and it takes a Christian community to form a Christian. Congregations need to examine their entire communal life and look at how what they do and the way they do it is forming children and youth (and, for that matter, the rest of the congregation). What do our young people learn from the act of excluding them from part of the worship service and from the primary ministries of the congregation? What would happen if we included baptized children and youth as catechists in baptismal preparation? Could we form "families" where older, experienced Christians would mentor younger families—and build relationships that could be a true expression of mutual ministry?

---

Children and youth need to participate fully in the central formative event of the church's life, its worship.
— Anthony B. Robinson

---

Children grow in faith and learn that their faith is important if they and their ministries are taken seriously by the church. Instead of shunting children off to their classrooms, applauding their occasional performances, or indulging their need for age-appropriate, often trivialized, activities, the church needs to incorporate children as full participants in the life of the church. That will not only help form children as faithful Christians, it will help adults grow in their faith as well. Children have a remarkable ability to see what is "really real" and speak the truth. They ask the questions that adults have long learned to avoid or ignore. They remind adults of what is essential, what is really important. Incorporating children into the life of the church will make the entire community whole and will engage the community in learning in a new way.

youth

Youth ministry has led the way in the use of what has been called "relational ministry" in the church. In the last century, youth ministry was largely focused on the need for youth to be "separate from" the congregation. Youth groups had their own room (often a "hole in the wall" room next to the boiler room). They had their own activities and went on their own trips. The assumption was that young adults, often not much older than the group members, were best equipped to lead the youth group. This "youth guru" was often someone who knew how to entertain young people. As long as the young people were having a good time and went to youth group meetings, the adults were happy. The adults often saw youth as alien creatures and were thus viewed with some discomfort, anxiety, and even fear. They hoped everyone would survive until the teenager grew up and could "reenter" civilized society.

Thankfully, in many churches today there is a much clearer recognition that youth are an integral part of the community. Relational youth ministry is based on the principle that young people come to know the love of God in Christ and what it means to be a Christian through an experience of being loved by adult members of the community who model the Christian life rather than just talk about it. In some cases there has been a shift from "programs" (an established curriculum) to "people." Even printed materials, such as the *Journey to Adulthood* (*J2A*) program are based in relationships, and assume that the materials will be used by the leaders more like a library than a course of study; in other words, they will be used to craft a process that is unique to every youth group. Mentoring programs have arisen as well as "processes" such as Mark Yaconelli's Youth Ministry and Spirituality

Project, which is designed to encourage adults in building relationships with youth.

CONTEMPLATIVE YOUTH MINISTRY
Mark Yaconelli is the son of Mike Yaconelli, the founder and former (now deceased) head of Youth Specialities, a publishing and consulting organization that generates a huge number of traditional youth ministry resources and programs. Mark grew up in the youth ministry culture and was himself a youth minister until he hit a wall. "I thought I was well-trained and well-equipped when I went to a church to run a youth ministry," he recalls. "It was a new, million-dollar facility. They gave me a big budget and interns. And after two years I was ready to quit. Youth ministry was killing me. I was working seventy to eighty hours a week. The kids weren't changing, none of them seemed very interested in what was going on, and the numbers were down. And because of all my time away from home, my marriage was in trouble."[18]

Yaconelli was the classic "youth guru" type of leader—young, male, talented, and eager to share his faith. When he finally faced the fact that it wasn't working, he went on retreat at a convent in Portland—not the usual setting for an evangelical Protestant! There he discovered contemplative spirituality. Asked to spend two hours in silence, reflecting on the Prodigal Son story, he realized that he saw God as constantly demanding more from him rather than welcoming him home—and he realized that more programs, more activities, and more lessons were not what he or his youth needed. "I know it might sound like a stupid, dramatic Christian story, but from that moment, everything in my life changed," Yaconelli stated. "When I came home, the first thing my wife said was, 'What happened to you?' She could tell *physically* that I was different. My shoulders weren't tense anymore. I had slowed down. I felt more alive. More myself. Less pressure.

More rest in what I was doing. And God was no longer just a philosophy or an idea or an expectation or a mission statement—God was a *very ordinary holiness.*"

From that point forward, Yaconelli began exploring how to invite youth into that sacred space and help them experience God as ordinary holiness. "First I decided to simply get out of the way. You see, I had this so-called 'relational youth ministry,' but it was as if my students had developed relationships with *me* instead of with God. I also started teaching my kids the ancient spiritual practices that I'd learned on the retreat."

Those of us in the Episcopal tradition might smile at his amazement at the power of silence, candles, prayer, and reflection, all of which is so central to our worship and prayer. But sometimes it takes someone from outside our own tradition to help us rediscover the power of those spiritual disciplines that are so very important in forming our relationship with God.

Yaconelli went on to teach at San Francisco Theological Seminary (Presbyterian), where he founded the Youth Ministry and Spirituality Project (YMSP), funded by a Lilly Foundation grant. YMSP continues as a group of Christians seeking to integrate Christian spirituality and youth ministry. They maintain a website which "comes from our desire to be a source of encouragement and inspiration to those who seek to welcome young people into the way of Jesus." It is also a site that provides a forum to share the research and experience of the Youth Ministry and Spirituality Project (YMSP), gathering "churches and youth ministers from across North America to explore contemplative prayer, discernment, spiritual direction, covenant community, spiritual practice and Sabbath-living as a way of re-sourcing ministries with youth."[19]

After working with youth for some time, Mark Yaconelli realized that adults need to learn the spiritual practices *first* so they could teach them to and model them for the youth. He now offers three annual Sabbath retreats for youth leaders that provide a time for adults who work with youth to learn how to stop, reflect, pray, and *be* with God instead of just telling youth *about* God.

SPIRITUAL FORMATION PROGRAMS

In other cases, the principles of relational youth ministry have been built into a youth ministry program, of which *Journey to Adulthood* is the prime example. It is based on the principles of both relational and contemplative youth ministry, but it also reflects a number of the other trends identified above, including experiential learning, educating the whole person, baptismal ministry, and grassroots resource development.

*Journey to Adulthood* (*J2A*) is a six-year program of spiritual formation originally developed by St. Philip's Episcopal Church in Durham, North Carolina and subsequently "grown" by users across the church. *J2A* is a complete youth ministry program of spiritual formation for sixth through twelfth grades. It uses Bible study, prayer, rites of passage, outreach ministries, and both serious and playful activities. There are three two-year segments of the program:

> *Rite-13:* The first two years (sixth and seventh, or seventh and eighth graders) focus on celebrating the individuality of each young person and his or her creative potential. The Rite-13 liturgy (A Celebration of Manhood and Womanhood) is the community expression of this. These two years also focus on building relationships and a sense of community—of "belonging" to the church as a whole.
>
> *J2A:* The middle portion of the program (eighth and ninth, or ninth and tenth graders) engages youth with the skills and critical thinking involved in adult-

hood. The youth plan and embark on a pilgrimage together at the end of this segment.

*YAC (Young Adults in Church):* A mentor-based program helping older teens (eleventh and twelfth graders) to discern and carry out a ministry within their church or in the larger community and to lead the congregation in a mission project. Vocation and development of a personal credo are also emphasized. The youth are responsible for choosing what to do and providing leadership.

Each group has in common a systematic focus on all the aspects of a whole person. Self, society, sexuality, and spirituality are covered in-depth in the first two groups. The exploration is done in the light of the gospel, "in order that the reality of young people's lives can be strengthened, encouraged, healed, corrected, and empowered by the life and wisdom of Jesus Christ."[20]

*J2A* began when a group of parishioners at St. Philip's came together in 1984. They recognized what many Episcopal churches were seeing: the traditional cycle of baptizing, educating, and confirming children wasn't working. Young people were leaving soon after being confirmed and, unlike previous generations, were not returning as adults. Confirmation had become an "exit ritual" for many youth. Meanwhile, during their time outside of the church, these young people were going through significant rites of passage: falling in love, getting their driving licenses, taking their first taste of alcohol, beginning to plan for their first job, and choosing a life partner. They were asking all sorts of questions based on ideas that they had never considered before. They were wondering what an ideal world, an ideal life, an ideal partner, an ideal God might look like. And the church was nowhere in their lives to help them reflect on those questions. The parishioners at St. Philip's wanted to change that. They developed a process that provided a way for young people to reflect on those questions in church, complete with rites of passage that were within the Christian community.

The parishioners at St. Philip's developed a series of notebooks containing the outlines of lesson plans and notes about their theories and experiences. When others heard about and asked for their program, they sought a grant from the Episcopal Church Foundation to hire Amanda Millay Hughes and David Crean to turn those notebooks into a curriculum. Since then, the original three hundred pages have grown into more than twelve hundred pages—a library of resources that includes several rites of passage (the most popular one being the Celebration of Manhood and Womanhood, nicknamed the Rite-13 liturgy because it is held near one's thirteenth birthday); Bible studies and activities; lessons focused on self, sexuality, spirituality, and society; a pilgrimage; mission projects; learning and practicing over twenty prayer methods; and ministry discernment and practice.

Manhood and Womanhood as gifts from a loving God may seem obvious to many of us. After all, we read in the first chapter of the book of Genesis, "God created humankind in his image, in the image of God he created them; male and female he created them." And more than that, God blessed them. Our gender—this wondrous gift from God—is an integral part of our blessed relationship with each other and with God.
— *Journey to Adulthood*

*J2A* integrates relational youth ministry, Christian formation, and spirituality into a holistic process. Instead of a one-size-fits-all set of workbooks that teens look at on Sundays, *J2A* provides a structure of how to relate to young people. The lesson plans and liturgies are offered in electronic files so congregations can adapt them to their own local community and arrange them in the order that allows them to create their own custom-made program. The materials can also be used as a "resource library" for those doing a self-designed process such as the Youth Ministry and Spirituality Project described earlier.

MENTORING PROGRAMS

Mentoring programs include adults mentoring youth and youth mentoring youth. The more traditional mode is adults mentoring youth—either using programmatic materials or in ministry. This is a model often used in confirmation programs where an adult meets with an individual young person to discuss faith issues. It is also a model used with older youth who are encouraged to work in a ministry with an adult already engaged in that ministry. The adult then takes on the responsibility of role modeling and may engage in reflecting on their ministry. In some cases it may also include curricular materials.

The Youth and Family Institute (Lutheran) has a peer ministry program that incorporates the principles of relational youth ministry, with the twist that the modeling comes from a relationship with a peer. Young people are involved in deciding what will be the focus of their learning sessions and they lead the sessions. Dr. Barbara Varenhorst is the leading pioneer for these peer programs, both with schools and churches. She helped develop the program at Youth and Family Institute (YFI). As a school counselor Varenhorst recognized that she and the excellent counseling staff at her school didn't begin to meet the needs of their students. When she asked students who they turned to for help, most students named peers. When she asked them, "When a friend comes to you with a problem, do you know how to help him or her?" the answer usually expressed a wish that they could be better at helping. So, working with the state of California, Barbara developed a written curriculum and began training what was then called Peer Counseling, followed by a host of additional programs. Varenhorst has been the main writer, advisor, and trainer of staff for the peer ministry program at YFI. She continues to encourage groups to seek training for adult facilitators since "peer ministry programs can only be as good as the training adults receive."[21]

Peer ministry assumes that youth are partners in ministry. It believes that if youth aren't leading, they're likely to be leaving! Peer ministry is about youth making, being and helping a friend—"relationships are ministry." While there are training programs for both adults and youth, peer ministry is itself not a "program" but rather a concept—the belief that youth can minister to other youth. The four elements in peer ministry are:

1. Quality training in caring skills.

2. Faith and values growth with purpose.

3. Christian service with people.

4. A lifelong attitude and practice.

The two key skills are:

1. Welcoming: Peer ministers develop a sensitivity to others who are not adapting or fitting in, making every effort to welcome and include others in all situations, promoting diversity and acceptance.

2. Caring: Peer ministers become aware of the hurts and needs of those around them living out the Good Samaritan story. They are available as caring listeners, guiding healthy and purposeful decisions, assisting others to learn the social skills, and referring to appropriate resources when needed.[22]

Youth are encouraged to integrate these skills into their lives—it is more about *being* than *doing*. So peer ministry is seen as something that happens with an individual as well as within the family, the congregation and the community. (See the Resource section at the end of this book for more information on peer ministry.)

WHAT'S NEXT?

Many churches are still doing a traditional, classroom-based Sunday school program with youth, where a Bible passage is studied or a current topic is discussed. As our children leave Sunday schools that have used multiple intelligences (such as the Workshop Rotation Model™), they are more and more likely to find this traditional model boring. If we hope to keep them engaged and involved in the life of the church, we will need to find other ways to do Christian formation with youth. The programs described above work well for the moment but we can always create additional programs and processes that help congregations form youth as disciples of Christ.

The "youth guru" model of entertaining young people apart from the community is still used in many churches. The problems with this model are manifold:

+ When the youth guru leaves, the program tends to collapse.

+ Youth only have an experience of one or two people and they are often young Christians who are still figuring things out for themselves.

+ Programs with only one primary leader are vulnerable to boundary violations or even sexual misconduct. While this can happen with multiple leaders present, it is not as likely as it is with one person as the focus of the young people's admiration.

+ These programs often provide more entertainment and inspiration than Christian formation.

+ The congregation loses the benefit of a holistic ministry that includes the participation of youth, who are often the best at honesty and inspired vision, good at smoking out hypocrisy, and are a real inspiration to tired adults.

+ This model often requires a paid youth ministry staff person that fewer and fewer churches are able to afford.

The focus on entertainment is best left behind. The church simply cannot compete with the entertainment being offered by the rest of the world. Our attempts at doing so only make us appear silly or boring. On the other hand, no other organization in society is as well equipped to teach our youth about God, Jesus, spirituality and prayer, or the Christian faith as we are. And we are also able to provide young people with meaningful opportunities to serve. Young people want to learn about and be in relationship God; they want life to be meaningful; they want to make a difference in the world. If the church doesn't provide those opportunities for them, other faith groups and secular service organizations will.

The church is likely to continue to see growth in the emphasis of having youth as full participants in the life of the church. This is supported by the conversation about baptismal ministry. As the number of small churches continues to increase, full inclusion will become more normative since small churches traditionally involve youth—often because there aren't enough for them to have a separate group. This trend, however, is likely to infuse the whole church.

As young people become more involved in the life of the church, we are likely to see an increased emphasis on spirituality and service—two aspects of the faith that are very important to youth and young adults. If we take them seriously (as we must), we will need to teach them how to pray and be in a deeply committed relationship with God in Christ—and for many adults, that will mean we need to learn how to do it ourselves. We also need to practice what we preach: young people will demand that of adults. That can be a real gift to the church that we should welcome and embrace.

Young people are likely to lead the way in developing online resources, websites, and audiovisuals. They are naturals in this arena and with some encouragement can teach the rest of the congregation how to use this medium to teach, learn, and communicate the gospel. This may be a place where peer ministry needs to move next: What would it look like to have young Christians writing blogs (or whatever is their successor) on issues of concern to youth, or finding ways to interact with their peers in a Facebook environment or developing clips to put on YouTube? What would happen if the church developed a global online virtual youth group? How might we encourage our youth to explore ministry and even evangelism using these mediums? What education, training, and support would they need? These are questions adults in the church need to begin discussing with youth so we can build a new vision for doing ministry with youth in the future.

----

## adults

Adults are more varied in their educational needs today than ever before. Some are biblically illiterate; others know the basic Bible stories but have no idea how to study the scriptures at any depth. Still others have come from denominations where they know the Bible very well, but have learned interpretations and approaches to the scriptures that are not compatible with Anglican theology. And, of course, some adults have taken classes in college, have a seminary degree, or have completed in-depth programs like Education for Ministry (EfM).

Adults have equally varied needs for spiritual formation. An increasing number of adults have not been baptized and have no church background. Others may have been baptized but have no real understanding of Christianity, much less of the Episcopal Church's theology, worship, and traditions. Some adults come from other denominations, faith groups, countries, or cultural backgrounds and bring those perspectives with them. Some have mastered "church life" but desire a deeper relationship with God and want a richer prayer life. Others have been lifelong Episcopalians, are steeped in the faith, and want to go deeper.

There are some things that the church, if it is to be the church, will always be engaged in doing. In many ways these are described by the classic marks of a church: *kerygma* (worship and celebration), *didache* (teaching and learning), *koinonia* (community and care), and *diakonia* (service and witness). — *Anthony B. Robinson*

When a congregation offers one or two adult faith formation groups, it will only meet the needs of a few adults. Many people either will be overwhelmed and confused by an approach that is too advanced for where they are, or they will bored with repeating something they have done several times before. Congregations need to offer many different options and encourage small groups (and individuals) to take responsibility for their own learning. Collect information on a range of programs and have them accessible so people can look at them. Set up a small table at coffee hour and offer a selection of books and videos/DVDs on a specific topic. Learn to be spontaneous—not all groups have to be planned ahead of time or need a curriculum, nor does every group need to meet for weeks and weeks. Groups can be formed throughout the year as the need or desire arises. They can even meet for just one time, and spur people on to further investigation on their own.

Above all, it is important to integrate learning into doing. Making learning a part of doing ministry makes the learning more relevant and more likely to be remembered. Look at every congregational activity and ask: Where can we build in learning opportunities? Not all learning has to be in fifty-minute classes or two-hour small group sessions. Weave learning into all of life. How we worship and work together, how we care for one another, and how we serve the world are all formational experiences—they all help make us who we are. Congregations need to be intentional about how faith formation happens through its living as well as in its formal teaching.

Incorporating learning experiences into ministry times can be informal and done without an established program. The choir can do a few minutes of Bible study and its relationship to the anthem during the choir rehearsal. Those engaged in a mission project can read a chapter of a book aloud, discuss it, and have prayer time together before or after their work. Eucharistic visitors can look at the lessons for the coming Sunday and plan a few words to say as a "homily" during their visits.

Focus on helping adults understand the importance of lifelong learning: set the norm (and repeat it constantly) that every adult needs to be in at least one disciplined process of faith formation. Provide opportunities and create ways for people to identify what they want or need and to find others who share those desires—match them with a choice of resources, programs, and suggestions. There are a host of programs and resources offered by all of the major publishers. Gather information on a wide variety of them and have that available so you can form groups as needed throughout the year. Start groups often and let the group decide when and where to meet and what to do. Make resources available and support anyone who is willing to serve as the coordinator. The church's responsibility in forming adult Christians is:

- ◆ to identify the resources (which includes programs, people, materials, and events) and make them available;

- ◆ to consistently hold up the norm that each person should be involved in at least one learning experience a week;

- ◆ to assist people in finding a group or a way to be engaged in learning; and

- ◆ to provide encouragement and logistical support (announcements, emails, refreshments, newsletter stories, and so on).

Small group programs based on experiential learning and relational ministry dominate adult faith formation today. The problem is not so much finding the programs, but deciding which programs to choose. And, more importantly, it is essential that the church take adult faith formation seriously and communicate the importance of lifelong learning to the congregation. Most congregations offer too few options, always hoping to find that one "magic bullet" that everyone will like while failing to make faith formation available in other ways than small group programs.

EXPERIENTIAL LEARNING

Most, if not all, of the small group programs are based on the concept that people learn best when they are in relationship with one another and are actively engaged in the learning process rather than just listening or reading. In addition to considering published programs or materials, you can of course design your own programs, using any source of content (book, audiovisuals, the newspaper, participants' experience or knowledge) or any event or ministry activity as the focal point. The basics are the same whether it is a learning opportunity you create or a program you adapt.

1. Identify your goals: what do you want people to learn? Is it specific knowledge, skills, or a process—or a combination of several of these?

2. Identify possible ways of presenting the information or skill or process you want people to learn. What are some ways of engaging people in exploring it?

The most important thing is to design some activity that invites people to *do* something—discuss questions; do an artistic, musical, or dramatic representation; write or say something; watch and try out an action. We almost always learn best when we *do* something, then reflect on that experience and draw conclusions about it that we can apply to the same or similar situations. That "experience, analyze, generalize, apply" cycle helps people integrate learning. Practice, preferably soon afterward, reinforces what one learns.

Use the same principles to evaluate a program as you do to design it. Look at the program's goals: do they fit what you want to accomplish? Make sure the program has some action, some way for people to "work with" the material. Even the rector's forum or other lecture formats can still be a useful model, as it is a good entry point for newcomers and attractive to those who do not like small groups (and not everyone does). With a good presenter and interesting topic, it can be a way to present information to a group quickly and easily. You can make it experiential simply by incorporating discussion and activities that engage people in doing something with the topic at hand. Something as simple and old-fashioned as having people look up passages in the Bible and read them aloud is a good example of an "activity" we might not think of as helpful today. But in a world where people don't read the Bible and have no idea whether Exodus is at the front or back of the book, getting people to use their Bibles (and encouraging them to own one and bring it with them) can be a useful teaching tool.

RELATIONAL MINISTRY

In a world where people's lives are increasingly fragmented and where even families don't have much time together, building relationships is crucial. Newcomers need to be invited to join a small group, though *not* one that is just a task that the church needs to be done! Study and prayer or spirituality groups are common options. Formation occurs in ministry groups as well, especially if group members are intentional about modeling, reflecting on, and applying what they learn to other aspects of their lives. Mentoring relationships, either one-on-one or in teams of three or four, are also good ways to build relationships. Each congregation needs to establish a way to help newcomers find a small group or other context where they can build relationships with others. We learn how to be a disciple of Christ largely by being in community—by seeing, hearing, and absorbing what it means to be a Christian.

For relational ministry to be effective it needs to provide opportunities for people to share their faith, pray together, and care for each other. Often churches think they have lots of groups for people to join, but these groups are often "task" groups that build relationships in a very superficial way and do not form people in faith. When relational ministry is working well, the group members turn to each other for support, for prayers, and for spiritual nurture in times of crisis and occasions of joy.

The goal in relational ministry is to find ways to build relationships that are significant and healthy. Because churches sometimes attract people who are needy and because they are groups of people who know they are supposed to be loving to all, they often become environments where boundaries are weak. This can lead to improper or inappropriate sharing (too much information), sexual misconduct, or domination by those who are mean (the parish bully), critical, overly sensitive, and hostile. Healthy relational ministry requires clear norms that are consistently enforced. While most congregations have some opportunities for relational ministry, few are intentional about it and even fewer can clearly identify who is in which group or other relationship—and who is missing.

## THEOLOGICAL EDUCATION BY SEMINARIES

One significant shift in the past fifty years has been the increase in the number of lay people who have chosen to attend seminary. Seminaries, which used to be almost exclusively devoted to preparing people for ordination, have expanded their offerings to appeal to laity. This trend is obviously motivated by the need for seminaries to generate income: seminaries have become more expensive at the same time that the number of ordinands has decreased, both because the Baby Boomer generation is no longer filling those seats at the rate they used to and also because almost half of all ordinands receive some or all of their seminary education at other denominational or ecumenical seminaries, graduate schools of religion, or in local self-study or group study programs. The recent changes to the ordination canons facilitates this trend, as well as a growing commitment to local formation that is more cost-effective, contextual, and (especially for more dioceses with a need for clergy to serve small churches) less likely to result in forming a seminarian for and creating a desire for a job in a large, suburban church.

A second motivation is the increased desire of laity for theological education that is available locally without requiring them to become full-time students. The Education for Ministry (EfM) program has both helped to meet this need and simultaneously to accelerate it. It provides theological education comparable to the first year of seminary offered in a local, small group context that usually meets once a week (a couple of groups even "meet" online). One result of the program is that it is not unusual for participants to head off to seminary after finishing four years of EfM. Some of them do so in response to a call to ordination, but others are committed to life in the church as a lay person. Meanwhile, seminaries are responding to the church's need for a more theologically educated laity by offering flexible residential programs that do not require moving to a seminary for three years and by taking their course offerings to the local settings by sending out professors or offering online courses.

SPIRITUAL FORMATION

Spiritual formation programs today range from the traditional prayer group to New Age practices. There is a renewal of interest in ancient traditions such as chanting, pilgrimages to holy sites around the world, and prayer methods developed by monastics. Programs have emerged to train people as spiritual directors—companions or guides for people who seek to develop a life of prayer. The General Theological Seminary in New York City offers a training program for those seeking to serve as spiritual directors or retreat leaders, as does the Shalem Institute for Spiritual Formation in Washington, D.C. In this multi-cultural, multireligious society many Christians have an increased interest in exploring other faiths and sharing or incorporating their faith practices into a Christian prayer life. This interest raises important questions for churches that encourage this exploration: if we say that "praying shapes believing," how will praying in ways that form one as a Buddhist or Hindu or Muslim form our belief as

Christians? If we merge or integrate beliefs of other faiths into Christianity, will we still be Christian? At what point does one say "this is Christian" and "that is not Christian"? On what basis does one make these decisions? These groups that focus on spiritual formation vary widely in the church today, but what they all have in common is a desire to help people find a deeper, sustained relationship with God.

While there are a multitude of programs, books, and other resources on spiritual formation available from publishers and program providers (see the Resource section at the end of this book), most churches create their own offerings in spirituality. Here is just a small sampling of the types of offerings you can find on the websites of various churches:

> *Yoga Class:* Yoga is a discipline that helps the body relieve stress and move beyond tension so that with greater self-awareness you might then be more receptive to God's voice within. This practice prepares the practitioner for meditation and inner peace.

> *Centering Prayer* is a method of reducing the obstacles to the gift of contemplative prayer and of facilitating the development of habits conducive to responding to the inspirations of the Holy Spirit. It is a way of cultivating a relationship with God and a deepening of faith in God's abiding presence within and in the world around us.

> *Beads of Prayer:* For many centuries, prayer beads have been used to deepen our relationship with God. Used as part of Contemplative Prayer, meditation, or a focused discipline, praying with beads leads us closer to the Divine. Learn how to pray while using the beads, alone and in groups, and

then lead others to do so as well. This is an activity open to all ages.

*Evenings of Ignatian Prayer:* These evenings offer an opportunity to explore a scripture-based method of prayer suggested by the *Spiritual Exercises* of St. Ignatius.

*Spiritual Direction:* Do you hunger to be closer to God? Individual spiritual direction is about learning to see how generously God is acting in your life, and about discerning how God might be inviting you to deeper relationship in loving response. Small group spiritual direction...offers a chance for individuals to deepen their prayer life and share their spiritual journey with others while growing in community.

*Way of Life Community:* Way of Life is a covenant community of two groups, Alpha and Omega, that provide sustenance, support and encouragement for the spiritual life and growth of its members. The groups seek to help each member be open to and able to discern God at work in everyday life.

At another congregation, what may well be a fairly traditional Bible study and discussion group is recast as spirituality and is thus likely to be more appealing, especially to younger women:

*Spiritual Care for Women:* This new group offers a coffee break for your soul. Its purpose is to give our spirits a morning jolt through Scripture, sharing and prayer. The on-going group begins a new topic every six weeks. Join any time.

Other prayer groups in that congregation focus on a survey of prayer forms:

*An experience of prayer:* Over the past 20 centuries, Christians have practiced their spirituality in a wide variety of forms. Come, learn and experience the richness and variety of Christian prayer, meditation and contemplation. A Spiritual Director will teach about these methods of prayer and lead the group in practicing and experiencing them.

Many groups in the church today recognize the power of twelve-step programs and seek to incorporate many of the principles found in those programs:

*Spiritual Support Group:* What contribution can you make and what benefit can you gain from the Spiritual Support Group that meets the second and fourth Sunday of each month? Come and find out. The meeting is based on the 12-step programs and includes readings, sharing and prayer.

This is just a small sampling of the creative and lively efforts churches are making today to provide formation in prayer and spiritual traditions. They are clearly designed to tap into the desire for spirituality so widespread in the world today. The question is: How do we, as the church, respond to this desire in ways that form people as faithful disciples of Christ, while avoiding the modern temptation for private and individualistic religious practices in which spiritual traditions become solely self-help methods for improving the quality of one's life?

ELECTRONIC MEDIA

In this electronic age there is a growing body of Christian formation resources available online, as well as on DVDs or other electronic media. One sign of this trend is the Diocese of Washington's website called the Episcopal Café (www.episcopalcafe.com), which offers daily readings in spirituality as well as various meditations and artistic expressions connected to the church year and current events. Another website, www.teforall.org, was constructed by the Ministry Development Office of the Episcopal Church with the participation of seminaries and others offering theological education. It is a compilation of links to theological education programs and resources for people of all ages. If you want to find an Anglican program or resource, go to this website and you can find just about anything! This is an example of how the power of the internet can make information easily available to anyone with a computer and internet access.

A wide range of excellent websites provide interactive experiences for individuals (and some could be used by groups). Beliefnet (www.beliefnet.com) probably is the largest spiritual site. It is an independent, multifaith site that is designed to help individuals "find, and walk, a spiritual path that will bring comfort, hope, clarity, strength, and happiness." It provides "devotional tools, access to the best spiritual teachers and clergy in the world, thought-provoking commentary, and a supportive community" as well as articles, quizzes, devotionals, sacred text searches, message boards, prayer circles, and photo galleries on an extremely wide range of topics.

Explorefaith (www.explorefaith.org) is an ecumenical site (although largely started and staffed by Episcopalians) that exists "to provide an open, non-judgmental, private place for ANYONE interested in exploring spiritual issues." It seeks to help people grow in faith "by providing rich and varied material about God, faith and spirituality." The website is "deeply committed to ongoing spiritual formation for people of all ages and all backgrounds, living in countries around the world." Explorefaith.org provides articles, meditations, podcasts, and daily hours of prayer that can be set to your time zone. This is one way to invite seekers and to support committed Christians in exploring their faith and practicing spiritual disciplines.

As with the plethora of small group programs and resources in spirituality being offered in the church today, the problem with electronic resources is not a dearth of offerings but confusion about which ones to choose. How can the church help Christians find and use these resources to enhance their learning? How can the church help them sort through what they find there, to reflect on what they are learning and decide what to keep and what to reject? And perhaps most critical, how can we help people who come to these sites find their way into a Christian community, where their formation can occur in relationship with others rather than just by interacting with a computer?

WHAT'S NEXT?

The primary thing that used to work but is not likely to work in most churches now is offering a single adult education experience for the faithful few. We can no longer afford to have just one or even two offerings a week and expect to meet the needs of an increasingly diverse adult population. We can't assume that people know the basics of the biblical story or the faith. We can't assume they understand the religious words we use—not even those that are common to those of us in the church. We can't assume that people who are attending are baptized or even that they are believing, much less practicing Christians. We have to assume that the people we see in church are very different in what they want and need— and we need to find ways to meet those diverse needs.

Most adult faith formation resources and programs are designed for middle-aged adults. The underlying assumption of these programs is that most adults have been raised in the church or have been active for some time. Most programs do *not* start at the very beginning... although there are more and more middle adults who need that. And they make many assumptions about what the participants already know—presuming a background in Christian formation that many adults today don't have. So, many of the program and resources available today need to be "translated" or have explanations embedded into them or provided by the leaders.

Churches can't assume that people will come to adult education offerings any more than they can assume people will come to church. Announcements, stories in the newsletter, or ads in the local paper are no longer effective in recruiting participants. You have to invite people one by one. Congregations need to find out what people want and need to learn to be a disciple of Christ, actively ministering in the name of Christ. They need to help adults of all ages understand why participating in an ongoing process of Christian formation is important for them.

It intrigued me to see how many of the congregations I visited had ministries serving the homeless. Many people mentioned that, despite the fact that they lived in houses, they too "felt homeless" and experienced a surprising kinship with the actual homeless people they befriended. Because of their own sense of dislocation, they felt that the homeless people had "taught" them about the spiritual life, trust, stewardship, healing, and commitment. — *Diana Butler Bass*

Congregations need to provide adult faith formation experiences that are not just relevant to participants but are also *quality* offerings. People today expect high quality, though that doesn't mean slick or expensive or complicated. It means offerings that are led by people who are skilled, prepared, and authentic. It means using learning methods that are contemporary and effective. It means providing offerings that are significant and meaningful. It means taking learning seriously.

"What goes around, comes around" is an old expression that might well be applicable to adult faith formation. I believe that old-fashioned Bible study is something we need to return to doing on a more regular and systematic basis. Because so many of our adults have "missed out" on Christian education during their childhood and young adulthood, many of them need basic Bible study. Others have received their understanding of the Bible in other denominations, or they stopped learning as a child and have a fifth- or sixth-grade understanding of the Bible. Clergy often worry about offending people by teaching them modern biblical scholarship, especially when it undermines people's understanding of the Bible as a simple story and rule book, so they fail to teach people how to engage in serious study of the scriptures.

A hallmark of Anglicanism is that we are the "thinking person's church." If we are to engage people's intellect, we need to develop a variety of ways people can learn to study the scriptures, using the tools of modern biblical scholarship. These ways need to use multiple intelligences and different learning styles, varied times and places, and different levels of understanding and readiness. But our goal should be to have a biblically literate congregation.

Because the experience and needs of adults today are so varied, I believe we need to look at ways of guiding adults in identifying what they want and need to learn and then in finding ways to meet those needs. Perhaps we need to train a cadre of "faith formation guides" (or "spiritual formation guides") who will help individuals and groups assess their needs, develop learning plans, and identify resources. So instead of offering a list of groups, events, and programs, leaving adults to pick and choose with little or no guidance or sense of direction, we might start by identifying what people want and need and *then* develop the list of what is being offered. This would help people move from one level of faith formation to the next rather, than just picking and choosing learning experiences at random. It also would communicate that the church is serious about adult faith formation and the importance of intentional lifelong learning. And it most likely would force us to hone our resources and programs to meet the needs of the people instead of being what they often are now—programs that we think people *should* have.

In the years ahead, I believe we will see more learning integrated into formation for ministry and in the practice of ministry. The church is most alive when people are transformed by Christ and are active participants in carrying out God's mission to restore people to God and each other in Christ (BCP 855). People learn by doing, and they are motivated to learn when they are engaged in something that matters to them. Helping people discern their call to ministry and preparing and supporting them in those ministries will become key arenas where learning occurs.

I also believe that congregations must become very intentional about integrating learning into worship. Praying really does shape believing, so how we pray together matters. This includes everything from the music we use to the way we proclaim the word of God. It includes the images we have around us and the significant symbols of the faith (baptismal fonts, chalice and paten, crosses). It includes how we act, what we say in the bulletins, and how we preach our sermons. In includes how we pray for healing, confess our sins, intercede for others, and offer the Great Thanksgiving. All of these form us as Christians. Congregations need to re-vision how to worship so their liturgy is truly forming people to be active, participating Christians. As Verna Dozier says: "Do you want to follow Jesus? Or are you content just to worship him?"[23] Congregations need to help people learn how to follow Jesus.

I would like to see congregations become learning communities—places where individuals "catch" the vision that we are all on a journey of learning and growing in the faith, places where the congregation as a whole learns and grows in the faith. The cycle of "experience, observe, reflect, analyze, generalize, apply" is a learning cycle that helps congregations grow instead of just repeating the same patterns over and over again. A congregation that expects itself to learn and practices the learning disciplines collectively will grow in faith. A congregation that sees itself as being on a journey of learning and that constantly reflects on what the congregation is learning creates an environment in which individuals see themselves as growing and learning.

While these points apply to adults of all ages, I want to briefly address specific age groups: young adults and older adults. These two groups, which are often ignored, have particular needs and perspectives that the church must recognize and address.

---

## young adults

The Episcopal Church has almost no program or curricular materials that have been developed specifically for young adults (ages eighteen to thirty-five) beyond college chaplaincies. This also is the age group that is least likely to be found in our pews on Sunday morning. Perhaps there is a correlation here?

Many young adults today have grown up outside the church (or any faith group). They are not likely to come to church unless invited by someone who knows them. Ironically, most young adults *would* accept an invitation from someone they know—but few are invited. And we can't expect them to arrive on their own. If you saw a family reunion at a local park, would you walk up and help yourself to lunch? Not likely. Most of us would never presume to invite ourselves into another family's event. Coming into a church building when you've never been to one before and don't know anyone there is equally intimidating for most young adults.

If and when young adults do arrive, most churches have nothing to offer that meets their specific needs. Young adults are especially responsive to spirituality and service, so providing opportunities in these areas is a good entry point. The church also needs to provide "the basics"—introductions to the faith and Bible. While many structured programs are available (see the Resource section), even a simple offering will do. Elizabeth Keaton, the rector at St. Paul's in Chatham, New Jersey, for example, regularly declares a "Reformation Month" and offers a free Book of Common Prayer to anyone who will sit with her while she describes what it is, how to use it, and how it contains what they need to know about the Episcopal Church's understanding of the faith. She finds that young people respond positively to this introduction to the faith and the Episcopal Church. Ideas like these are what congregations need to explore as they look for ways to invite young adults into life in Christ.

Many of the examples of programs listed in the Resource section at the end of this book will work with young adults. In some congregations, all groups will be mixed in age; in others young adults may prefer to be involved in a group of people their own age, with their own program. Talk with people to see what their needs are and what appeals to them. You might establish groups by age—or you might establish them by "needs" (everyone who wants "the basics" might be in the same group, for example). Meanwhile, there are many other options that congregations can explore. Here are some ideas for things that might appeal especially to young adults.

## MILLENNIUM DEVELOPMENT GOALS
## AND U2CHARISTS

A popular cause at the moment is the Millennium Development Goals. This is a natural for young adults, as it appeals to their desire to make a difference and the global aspect resonates with their reality. Episcopalians for Global Reconciliation have a host of resources you can use to launch or support work in this arena (www.e4gr.org).

A complementary movement has started that also appeals to young adults: U2charists. U2charist is an Episcopal service of the Eucharist that features the music of the rock band U2 and a message about God's call to rally around the Millennium Development Goals. U2charist was conceived by Sarah Dylan Breuer in 2003, with the first public service held in 2004 in Baltimore, Maryland. Breuer was inspired to create the U2charist by the publication of *Get Up Off Your Knees,* a collection of sermons using U2's lyrics that was published by Cowley Publications in 2003. After the Maryland services, other churches began holding such services, and at the end of July 2005 Paige Blair, rector of St. George's Episcopal Church in York Harbor, Maine, led her first U2charist, to which over 130 people came. After holding three U2 services, including a baptism, in 2006 the people of St. George's began mentoring other churches, and what began as an Episcopal Church experience has become a worldwide movement. Blair describes the U2 services in this way:

> The liturgy itself is pretty traditional—it has all the usual required elements: a Gospel reading, prayers, and communion from an authorized prayer book. The music is really what is different. And yet not so different. It is rock, but it is deeply and overtly spiritual. One element that is very important is our using this opportunity to teach people about the Millennium Development Goals to eradicate

extreme poverty and global AIDS. Facts about extreme poverty are included in the PowerPoint slides, particularly during the instrumental parts of songs. The sermon is designed to raise awareness, as well as empower the congregation to take action and do their part to make poverty history (such as signing the ONE Declaration).[24]

Along similar lines, Episcopalians for Global Reconciliation also has a *Youth Action Guide* designed for young people under twenty-five years of age. It can be downloaded to start a conversation with young adults (see www.e4gr-more.org/mdgyouthactionguide.pdf). *Youth for a Sustainable Future* is a guide on how to organize a youth summit (see www.e4gr-more.org/ysfguide.pdf).

### THEATRICAL THEOLOGY

One of the best ways to engage young adults (and adults of all ages, for that matter) is to use "stories" offered by the culture. Movies, plays, and television programs are all easily available, and the production quality is almost always far superior to whatever the church could afford to produce. In addition, the secular culture markets their offerings so all we have to do is pay the ticket price to get a good "discussion starter." Our expertise is not in production methods—it is in helping people think theologically.

St. Paul's Episcopal Church in Chatham, New Jersey, offers an annual "Theatrical Theology" series that seeks to do just that. Elizabeth Keaton describes what happened when the group of about twenty-five members viewed the movie *The Valley of Elah,* which she found to be "a deeply disturbing film about war—its history in the course of human events—and heroism—its complexity and imperfection. . . . On a deeper level, it is a psychodrama about how it is we deal with the presence of evil and those we consider 'monsters' in our midst."

After viewing the film at the theater some of the group met to "decompress" with a discussion at a local restaurant, while others chose to do so alone, through meditation and prayer. The next day Keaton led a discussion at the church, beginning with an overview of ethics in general and Christian ethics in particular to set the context for the discussion. She then outlined questions to guide the discussion about the film:

1. What is (are) the major ethical issue(s) of this film?
2. What is the "right thing" to do in this film—especially in terms of any tension you see between secular and Christian ethics?
3. Who was the "hero" in this film? Who displayed both courage and self-sacrifice? What, if any, is the difference between the Christian hero and the hero of the secular humanist?
4. Where is God in this story?
5. What is the moral of this story?
6. What, if any, cultural considerations impact our understanding of morality, heroism, and theism?
How are you changed by this story? This discussion? What might you do differently because of your ethical reflections?

This is a simple model for how a congregation can engage younger and older adults in a dialogue about a movie, play, or television program. It's fairly easy, low cost, and can be effective Christian formation. As Keaton says: "I do believe that the church is at its best when she challenges and deeply engages the community in discussions about important questions of our time. I would encourage you to take the risk and begin a series like this in your own community of faith. This is our third year and we have found it to be a wonderful adult educational series as well as a great evangelism tool."[25]

The Episcopal Church used to have a very strong and effective campus ministry program. One result of the financial strains faced by all of the mainline denominations has been the cuts in funding for campus ministry. Many faithful campus ministers, dioceses, and congregations near campuses have struggled to continue the campus ministry tradition. But I suspect that some of the disappearance of young adults is directly attributable to the cutbacks in campus ministry. College is a time in the lives of young adults that is turbulent and formational. Campus ministries are there to help students during this time and give them an experience of the Christian community that sustains them in the transition from adolescence to adulthood.

We used to assume that while most young adults might leave the church when they finished high school (or after confirmation) and spend some time "finding themselves," they would return with the birth of their first child. For many reasons, this is no longer happening. Young adults are still leaving but they are not returning. Assuming that the birth of a child or some other precipitating event will bring them back is not going to work. We need to develop intentional practices of inviting young adults and providing programs, groups, and resources that meet their needs.

We also have assumed that all adults look alike and have the same needs. While the entire adult generation is becoming increasingly diverse, this is especially true for young adults. Young adults today have been raised in the technological age of the postmodern world—they see and experience the world differently from adults raised in the machine age of the modern world. One worldview is not particularly better or worse than the other, but the reality is that they are profoundly different. We cannot keep repeating what we've done before and expect a different result—we need to find new ways.

Some of what the church could offer young adults is in traditional programs. Parenting groups would appeal to those with children. Singles groups or young adult groups would be helpful in churches with large numbers of those populations. Practical workshops on budgeting, dealing with stress, and other issues of concern to young adults could be offered to the larger community as an entry point. So would offerings that explore cultural entertainment mediums from a theological perspective (like Theatrical Theology series). If young adults are drawn to spirituality and are going to the local gym or ashram for yoga training, why not have yoga and meditation groups meeting at the church? All of these are ways to help young adults in their faith formation journey—but most or all of them are missing from the vast majority of our congregations. We can't do them all, but we must do some of them if we expect young adults to be full participants in the church.

The Generation Xers (1964 to 1976) are a small cohort group coming behind the Baby Boomers (the largest cohort group in history). They have, as a consequence, been overshadowed by the Boomers but have been quite vocal and assertive in seeking their place in the church. However, that group is now beginning to leave the young adult stage and enter middle adulthood, where the primary leadership of the church traditionally has been focused. They are followed by the next, much larger, generation (1977 to 1998), which has grown up entirely in the internet era. This generation is individualistic, finds institutions irrelevant, and likes to rewrite the rules. They like to develop their own resources online, build their own networks and relationships, and maybe even develop their own "churches."

As we move into this next phase of the church's life, I believe it is even more important that older adults be intentional about building relationships with younger adults. There is much we can learn from one another and young adults have much to offer the traditional church. We also need to support their efforts at "reinventing church." If we don't find ways to make the gospel relevant to younger adults, we will continue to decline both as an institution and as a Christian movement. However, my guess is that young adults and those who work with them can and will start a new movement, though it may not be the institutional church as we are accustomed to, as I suspect that new times will bring new forms of being church.

Here is an example of the innovative possibilities the church needs to consider. Last Sunday I attended a service of Evening Prayer at the Anglican Cathedral in Second Life, a virtual world where you assume a character and interact with others through that character. There are two Sunday liturgies, Compline on Sunday evening, and a room in the crypt below where you can read the daily offices during the week. A bulletin board offers community announcements and allows you to leave notes for others, while an offertory box near the door accepts contributions. A global community of over two hundred Anglicans belongs to this Cathedral.

Time zone differences meant that I was doing Evening Prayer at 2:00 p.m. I "entered" a totally traditional Gothic cathedral and took my seat a bit early—since I was inexperienced I tended to walk into walls and trip over chairs so didn't want to make a fool of myself. I sat in the back and waited. A couple of minutes before the service about fifteen people came into the cathedral, took seats, some bowing to the altar before doing so, several of them chatting with each other in the familiar way one does in church. The "chats" were occurring in instant messages on the bottom left side of my screen. The bulletin I had picked up on my way in was open on the top left side of the screen.

Soon the minister started the service. He typed in his lines, and people responded—which meant that I saw "And also with you" flash by about eight times! At the time of the sermon, the minister (who, I decided, probably was in Australia) told us to hit "play," and I heard him preach a traditional sermon. We then finished the service as usual and about half of us went to the very attractive parish hall next door, where we sat in comfy chairs and discussed the story of Zaccheus.

What struck me as interesting about the whole experience was that it was on the one hand remarkably familiar. The greetings, liturgy, discussion, even the fact that all but one of us who went to Bible study were female—all were exactly what one would expect in church. Yet on the other hand we were gathered from all around the world—one woman was in London, another in New Zealand, and I in America—and interacting with each other using virtual characters in a virtual space. It was nonetheless a community of people who gathered weekly for an hour or two to worship and learn together.

This probably isn't the church of young adults—my guess is that the participants were largely Baby Boomers who were clergy or hoping to become clergy. But virtual communities are an indication of the type of experience that is attractive to young adults, and that the church needs to explore. A recent ad by a diocese in England sought a priest willing to start a virtual church. This and other experiments in online faith groups may, over time, begin to form and inform the church as a whole.

The differences between those who grew up in the modern and postmodern worlds mean that the church must be willing to present the gospel to young adults in new and different ways than those it used in the past. We need to think of how to take the gospel to the people, instead of assuming that the people will come in the church doors. We need to build relationships with young adults, to listen to them and honor how they see the world. We need to be willing to take some risks and try some new ways of engaging young adults in the process of faith formation. And perhaps most importantly for older adults, we need to recognize that young adults are actively, eagerly seeking to be in relationship with God. They may not be loyal to denominations or value the institutional church, they probably don't really care very much about our conflicts and issues, but they are often passionate about their faith and their desire to know God at profound levels. Older adults might be surprised to discover that the passion, commitment, spirituality, and faith of young adults, some of whom have never set foot in a church building, could be the spirit and energy that revitalizes the church.

### older adults

Like young adults, this group has very few programs or resources available that are developed to meet their specific needs. If you do a search on the internet for Episcopal resources for older adults, you're more likely to get a list of retirement homes than programs or ministry groups (the Episcopal Society for the Ministry on Aging dissolved in 2003). Most adult education programs are designed for middle adults and older adults patiently participate in them—even if they have already done similar programs multiple times before.

The author of *Godly Play*, Jerome Berryman, is developing a version of *Godly Play* for older adults in nursing homes. The process of telling the biblical story, asking "wondering" questions, and inviting a tangible response using art and objects works with adults who no longer have the ability or desire to sit through the long discussions of traditional adult education programs. Our oldest adults need to hear God's story and be given a way to respond that allows them to speak from the heart. *Godly Play* is likely to give us a way to proclaim the Good News to our oldest adults.

*Do the Right Thing* is a case-study program on ethical decision-making designed by and for older adults. The authors are members of the Academy of Senior Professionals at Eckerd College (ASPEC) in St. Petersburg, Florida, a continuing education program where professionals offer courses to other retirees. This course has been popular for several years, with new case studies introduced to the class and added to the resource. The program (available from www.LeaderResources.com) has a wide range of case studies on issues confronting older adults and their families. While it can be used with just older adults, it also works in groups with mixed ages.

WHAT'S NEXT?

We used to be able to comfortably assume that all adults from age thirty to eighty had the same educational and formational needs. We can't make that assumption any more. Older adults have different needs from younger adults, especially if we are successful at attracting more young adults who arrive with little or no background in church life. Also, older adults have different life experiences and concerns that are generally ignored by the standard adult programs. They may also have different spiritual needs.

The other assumption we have often made is that older adults either don't need or want education, or that they are content with a midweek Eucharist followed by a traditional Bible study led by the priest. The church needs to realize that the Baby Boomers are coming! The largest, as well as the most highly educated and active, cohort group in history is entering the older adult population. The church needs to be prepared for a group of older adults who will *not* be content with the traditional midweek service and Bible study. Older adults are likely to be highly active in ministry and will want and need education and support as they undertake ministries that are new to them or that they choose to engage at a deeper level than they could before retirement. These older adults also will bring a wealth of information, skills, and experience, so they will have much to offer as teachers and leaders as well.

Older adults today live longer, and are more active and involved in their communities than ever before. They are just as interested in learning and growing as younger adults. As this population grows in the church, we need to address their specific needs while simultaneously encouraging and inviting them to be part of intergenerational groups where they can share their wisdom and perspective.

The church needs to find ways to engage older adults in learning and in ministry. If we fail to do so, we will soon see the same phenomena we have with young adults—they will become involved in other leisure and service activities outside the church. Of course, this might well be exactly what the church needs: older adults, actively engaged in ministry in daily life, intentionally bringing the gospel to others and inviting them into the community. Most people come to church because someone they know has invited them. We need people dedicated to building relationships and living intentional lives of serving God, people who will open the doors of the church to those who would not enter without a companion's invitation and accompaniment. It may well be that our older adults will become our church's gentle evangelists if we can help them envision this ministry and empower them to do it.

Another reality that I believe will have an impact on the church is the Church Pension Fund's decision to offer clergy an "early retirement" option. The "55/30 and out" rule was instituted a couple of years ago. This means that clergy who are fifty-five years of age and have thirty years of service receive their full retirement benefits. These are the Baby Boomer clergy—large numbers, highly active, and unwilling to sit in their rocking chairs for the rest of their days. What might they want to teach or learn? Will they lead learning experiences in local churches? Will they create programs and resources they wish they had had when they were the rector, now that they have the time to do so? How can the church engage these clergy in the years ahead?

Finally, we need to give some thought to our ministry with our oldest adults. As the Baby Boomers age, they will move into retirement communities and nursing homes. Their large numbers mean they may no longer need to "go to church" by traveling to the local church. They are likely to be able to "do church" for themselves in their own communities—a pattern we are already seeing emerge. Many of these retirement communities, especially if they are affiliated with the church, will have Episcopal clergy living there who are willing to celebrate a weekly Eucharist and help organize learning and service opportunities for residents and the community. Will the church become more age-segregated as older adults, generally the stable population of local churches, meet their spiritual needs in their own environments? How will this affect the local church? What will our children, youth, and younger adults learn from the wisdom of our elders? How might we re-vision being the church, living and learning our faith in this new world? In other words, how can we find new ways of making disciples?

chapter five

# A New Vision
# of Discipleship

It is a bright fall day and Emily is on her way to church.
This is *not* a normal activity for her—in fact, Emily has
never been to a church before. But her friend Jon invited
her to join him for lunch and since he's been talking about
what a great time he has at this church, she's decided to
come along.

As she approaches the church, she notices lots of
people coming and going. Children are playing on the
sidewalk and in the tiny courtyard, while a couple of
groups of adults are standing around chatting. A noonday
concert has just finished in the main church building and
those people are leaving while others are arriving at the
building next to the church. Some of them are carrying
what she guesses is food for the lunch. She follows them
into the building and looks around for Jon.

"There you are," he says enthusiastically. "How about
helping me chop these onions? I'm in charge of making
my famous spaghetti sauce today," he explains. Someone
shows her where to put her purse and gets her an apron,
knife, and chopping board, and she's soon chopping

onions along with the rest of the crew. The conversation flows easily and everyone seems to have something to do. She notices a couple of other folks who wander in looking lost and sees that they too are welcomed and put to work.

There's companionable bantering and lots of laughter but Emily notices that there are also a few people who seem to be paying careful attention to making sure everyone is involved and engaged. One man catches her attention when he approaches the chopping station and picks up a knife. He looks like a street person, but seems to be right at home here. Nonetheless, almost immediately another man shows up at his elbow. "Hey, Bill," he says, "I really need some help over here. Can you give me a hand?" Bill looks a bit disoriented for a moment while the second man gently takes the knife out of his hand and ushers him to another part of the kitchen. The knife is passed to a woman who quickly puts it into a drawer, giving a couple of other people a knowing glance. Emily wonders what that was all about.

Lunch preparations are finishing up; it's time to set the tables and set out the food. A bell rings in the distance and suddenly there are people—especially children—coming from everywhere. She had seen children working on what looked like an art project in one corner of the room and the sound of singing in the distance. A troop of youngsters emerges from that direction along with several adults. Everyone pitches in to help set tables and assemble the meal. "Here, you can help me do the forks," one little girl says to another. The girl looks to her father for approval and when he nods, she joins in. "She's usually so shy, I'm surprised she's getting into it so quickly her first time here," he says softly to Emily. "Yes," she replies, "but this is such an easy group to join. It's my first time too," she adds, introducing herself. "Would you like to help me get this sauce onto the serving table?"

When everything is set up, a small bell rings and silence descends on the group. One of the teenagers starts singing softly, and is almost immediately joined by the others. Emily doesn't know the song but it is a simple and repetitive song of thanksgiving so by the time they get to the second time around she joins in. The song ends and bedlam breaks out as everyone scrambles to fill plates and find places to sit. For the next half-hour or so the group enjoys the meal and conversation. While there doesn't seem to be anyone in charge or any agenda, Emily notices that everyone is included and that the conversation has a different character to it than what she is accustomed to in other contexts.

Emily struggles to put her finger on what is different. As she looks around the room she sees every size, shape, age, and color of person imaginable. She looks at the people sitting at her table and tries to guess who they are. A well-dressed, well-spoken woman named Laura is across from Emily. Next to her is an elderly woman who is deep in conversation with the teenaged boy next to her. At the end of the table are a couple of guys who are not especially well-dressed, but one them, Bob, seems to take responsibility for asking interesting questions. She wonders if he is "in charge" of her table in some way.

On her side of the table is a family with two small children and a middle-aged lesbian couple who are taking the role of "auntie" with the children. One of them is helping the older child use crayons to draw on the paper tablecloth and asking the child questions about the boat and animals he has drawn. At one point the entire table gets into a conversation about animals. "I wonder," says the man at the end of the table, "what animals think about God." "They know that God loves them just as much as God loves us!" declares the little artist. That launches a conversation about the relationship between God and animals that leaves Emily wondering. "I wonder if animals do have a relationship with God, and whether God cares about animals—and what difference it makes," she thinks to herself.

As the meal is finishing up people start doing the dishes and cleaning up the dining room. Jon comes across the room. "Sorry for abandoning you," he says to Emily. "I was just fine," she replies. "We had an interesting conversation about God and animals." "Okay," he says, giving her a quizzical look. "Do you want to stay for the service?" "Sure," she replies, shrugging her shoulders, not sure what she is getting herself into.

Emily notices that those who had appeared earlier with musical instruments are now assembling at one side of the room, and soon they strike up a tune. The children gather around the musicians and start singing enthusiastically. Some of the songs are clearly their favorites and are even a bit silly. But gradually they settle into a couple of songs with enough words that song sheets are required and distributed. By this time, clean-up is finished and everyone gathers around to join in the last couple of songs. Emily notices a few others who had slipped into the room during the clean-up time, and they too join the group. During the last song, the musicians, with a teenager carrying a cross, lead the way into the church. Emily finds herself swept into the somewhat unruly procession.

As they enter the church, the musicians lead the way around a central altar platform and then take their places. Some people take seats in the chairs that encircle the altar while others stand along the back or go to retrieve large pillows or mats from piles around the room. Emily takes a seat with Jon and watches with amusement as the children and a few of the adults join in a joyful circle dance around the altar. A drum sets the beat and people around her are clapping, singing, laughing, and generally having a good time. This is *not* the image of church that Emily has in her mind, although she has to admit that, never having been in a church before, she really didn't know what to expect.

The dancing song winds to a close and the dancers and others begin to take seats in chairs or on the floor. Some sit around the edges of the room, others stand. Suddenly Emily is startled to hear a huge gong sound. She looks around and sees the large, Chinese gong off to one side. At the sound of the gong, everyone becomes silent, even the smallest children. A number of the children and teenagers, along with a few adults, are sitting in a lotus position on the floor around the altar. A few people kneel while others stand holding their hands at their sides with their palms upward and their eyes closed. Off to one side Emily sees three men kneeling on a prayer mat with their foreheads to the ground. Emily doesn't quite know what this is about, but it is clearly a time when everyone gathers themselves in the quiet. "I guess they're praying," she says to herself, not exactly knowing what that would mean. But she senses the presence of holiness as she sits in the silence. The gong sounds a second time. No one moves except the three men, who stand, bow, and then kneel again. Another minute goes by and the gong sounds again. This time people gradually begin to move around, relaxed while they wait for what will come next. Emily waits with them.

From somewhere behind her a man starts a strangely eerie chant in a language Emily doesn't know or under-stand. "*Shema, Israel, Adonai, Elohanu, Adonai echad,*" he chants, and the people repeat it back to him. Emily doesn't know what the words mean but she feels it as a call—and it draws her attention to an elderly man with a shock of white hair who is taking a place in front of the altar. There is a rustle of low-key excitement and she can see the expectant faces of the children, some of whom now come up to sit on the floor in front of him. They wait. And then the elderly man begins. He has a booming voice and an uncanny ability to tell a story in a way that is mesmerizing. Today the story is about a man named Noah, an ark, the animals, a flood. Emily remembers the boy drawing a boat and animals at lunch—was that what he was drawing? she wonders.

When the story is finished the man and people repeat the opening chant while the elderly man returns to his seat and silence descends. Finally the man who had sat at her table at lunch speaks. "I wonder what the animals thought about God," he says. Silence. "I wonder whether Noah was afraid to do what God asked him to do," says a young girl. "I wonder whether God caused the rain to fall or whether it was like our making our world go crazy with what we are doing with global warming and all that," says a teenaged boy.

Several more people speak and then a teenaged boy stands up and starts walking toward the altar as the musicians and people sing "Alleluia, alleluia, alleluia," over and over again. The boy picks up a large, decorated book from the altar and holds it over his head while he walks slowly around the altar. Everyone stands up. Some people bow as he passes by, some cross themselves, others raise their arms as if they are lifting the book upward. The boy stops in front of the altar with the children who are sitting there standing on either side. He opens the book. "The Holy Gospel of our Savior Jesus Christ," he announces solemnly. "Glory to you, O Christ!" the people respond.

"Jesus said," begins the boy as he spoke the words of Jesus. "Jesus said that not everyone who called him Lord would be united with God at the end of time, but only those who do God's will." He goes on to tell a story about one man who built on sand and another on solid ground. At the end he says that people were amazed because Jesus spoke with authority.

Emily can't exactly tell if he is reading the words or telling them, but she feels like this young man *knew* what

Jesus had said and is telling her and the people something very important. Emily, who has a brother about that age, is struck by how strong and authoritative this boy sounds. She wonders if her brother cared enough about anything to be that sure of himself in front of a group of people like this. But before she could think about much more, the boy finishes and returns the book to the altar, and then takes his seat.

A mother with a baby stands up and walks to the front of the altar, handing the baby to the children gathered at her feet. A couple of them lay the baby on a mat on the floor beside them while the other children settle down to listen. The woman begins talking about what Jesus had said and the Noah story. Before long, others chime in with comments or questions, including a couple of questions from the children that are rather interesting. Emily watches the woman as she talks, guides the dialogue, summarizes, and elaborates on what people are saying.

Emily doesn't really understand too much of what they are talking about, but she does understand that these people feel that God wants them to hear and do God's will, even when it is difficult or seems crazy, like the idea of building an ark on dry land! At one point the adults are telling of times when they have followed God's will, when the teenaged boy who had read the words from Jesus stood up. "Remember," he says, "Paul told the church in Rome that everyone sins and doesn't do what God asks them to do. So I think before we get too satisfied with ourselves, we need to look at all the ways we don't do what God wants us to do. Just this week Congress voted to open up yet another front in the war and I don't hear us saying anything about God calling us to be peacemakers." The leader-woman smiles. "Thank you for calling us back to our mission in the world, Dave," she says. "One of the gifts of our young people is that they are so aware of where we fall short and they have such a beautiful vision of what could be if we would love and serve God with all our heart and all our soul and all our mind."

Emily's mind wanders while the woman finishes the time of dialogue. "I wonder what the world would be like if we really did do what God asks us to do," she muses. "I wonder if God asks everyone—even me—to do something. I wonder what that would be and what my life would be like if I did it." She comes out of her thoughts in time to hear the woman invite everyone to prayer; she then returns to her seat while the musicians start another song. Two of the children scamper off and then come slowly down the aisle with a large icon of Jesus, which they set on the altar for everyone to see. Meanwhile, someone sets a small bowl on one side of the icon and drops some incense on the burning coal in it. Another adult helps a child light a candle that is placed on the other side of the icon. During these preparations people again settle into prayer postures similar to those Emily saw earlier in the service. This time, however, three people take small jars from the altar and stand as if they are waiting for something.

As the song fades away, a man stands and begins to chant a sentence while the people sing, "Christ, have mercy" in response and then hum while the man chants another sentence. Emily feels shivers go down the back of her neck—she doesn't know why, but the sound drew her into a place deep inside of her. When the chanting ends, the man invites people to pray for those who are ill or in trouble. All around her she hears the murmur of voices saying the names and sometimes the illnesses of people they know. She notices that the children join in naming the people they know, including one little boy who prays earnestly for "George, my dog, who is really, really sick and might die." Meanwhile, people are coming up to those who had taken the jars from the altar and who are now laying their hands on the heads of those who come forward and are anointing them. This continues for some time as the man asks for prayers for the church...for the world...for those who had died. Each time the murmur of voices rises, and then falls to silence.

Finally, the teenaged boy who had read the words of Jesus stands up and says, "My brothers and sisters in Christ, let us confess our sins against God and one another" as he turns and kneels before the altar. Some people kneel while others stand and bow their heads, and then they all join the young man in a prayer. During the prayer, Emily notices a man approaching the altar and putting a stole around his neck. At the end of the prayer, he stands next to the young man and declares that God has forgiven everyone. Then he invites people to stand and share the peace.

Emily isn't sure what that is, but all around her people are smiling, shaking hands or bowing to each other while they say, "God's peace," or just, "Peace." Emily shakes hands with a few people but is mostly aware of the fact that she does, in fact, feel much more "at peace" than she can remember feeling in a long time. Jon leans over and whispers, "How are you doing?" "Fine," she whispers back, thinking, "I've got a few questions to ask when this is all over!"

Before Emily realizes what is happening the musicians strike up a lively song and someone passes her a sheet with the words and music. As she joins in, she notices that the children have scattered around the room and are gathering baskets that have been set at various points around the room. Some of them contain money, lots of them have cans and boxes of food, one has shoes, and another looks like it is a laundry basket full of clothes. Some of the children are carrying toys, while others have books and school supplies. The children are forming a line and begin to parade up one aisle, around the altar, down the next aisle, and around and around, singing and dancing—and occasionally being given an extra can of food or money as they go by the people. At the end of the line are two older children, one proudly holding a stack of pita breads that Emily recognizes as having been baked earlier to be part of lunch, while the other carries pitchers with water and wine.

Eventually this happy parade ends up at the altar where the children arrange the overflowing baskets around the base of the altar and the bread and wine are put on the altar. The teenaged boy who read the Jesus words pours the wine into a large wine glass and adds some water before a woman with a stole steps to the center of the altar. Meanwhile, the people have started gathering around the altar. Some of the children find their parents while others look for a favorite friend. Emily and Jon join the throng. Someone hands Jon a booklet and suddenly he remembers that Emily doesn't know what is going to happen. So he finds the page and shows it to her. "You can follow the words if you like," he says, "or just listen. Either way is fine." Emily takes the booklet mainly because she wants to take it home to check it out later.

A woman begins speaking and everyone responds. She raises her arms and speaks the first paragraph. Then someone standing at the side of the altar reads the next part. Then the congregation joins in. It seemed to be some very special prayer that they said and even sang together. "AMEN!" everyone says loudly, startling Emily, who hadn't anticipated that. Then they say another prayer together and the woman tears one of the pita breads in half while the people sing a song. Then the woman passes the bread to someone near her and that person eats a small piece, and then passes it to the next person while the woman starts another piece of the bread with someone else. There isn't any real order to it but somehow the bread and wine are passed from one person to the next.

Emily isn't sure what she ought to do as the bread comes closer to her. "Emily, the body of Christ," Jon says, offering her a small piece of the bread. "Amen," she replies, taking and eating the bread.

Emily doesn't understand what it is about, but she can tell that this is the most important part of their time together. And she can sense God present in a way she has never experienced before. She knows that she will be back to eat and learn what these people know about God and perhaps learn what God knew about her.

The man with the stole who declared God's forgiveness stands in the back near the door, and everyone turns to face him, while the children and some of their parents gather around him. "Let us share news about our service in the world," he says. "Dr. Vardhan couldn't be here this morning but asked me to announce that he will be facilitating a conversation on medical ethics on Wednesday at 7:30 p.m. in the community room at the hospital. He would welcome others who would like to help him engage medical practitioners in this conversation." A couple of others stood to ask for help in organizing a community recycling effort on Saturday and for support in challenging a workplace practice that was discriminatory. "Go in peace to love and serve the Lord!" declares the teenaged boy who had read the gospel. "Thanks be to God!" the people respond and then they move out of the sanctuary into the street outside.

As Jon and Emily are about to leave, the man from Emily's table who asked the question of what animals thought about God approaches. "I hope you'll come back next week," he says with a wide grin. "I'm going to be baptized!" "Thanks," Emily replies. "I think I will," she says with a glance at Jon. As they walk down the street Emily asks, "Who is that guy? Isn't he one of the church leaders? I mean, he was leading the discussion at our table and all." "Oh, he *is* a leader," Jon replies. "He's been around for quite awhile now and really does a lot for the church. He's one of the residents at the homeless shelter we have." "Homeless!" Emily replies, rather shocked. "Yes, he's been living with us for the last couple of years in the winter months but he's on the streets in the summer. But it's really neat that he's decided to be baptized," Jon replies. "Baptized," Emily thinks to herself. "Whatever that means. Something else we'll have to talk about later. Or maybe I'll learn more next week...."

---

six months later...

Emily and two of her friends, Petra and Latifah, are back cooking the noon meal at Grace Church—something they do most Sundays. They had joined Emily when she started talking about serving the homeless and older people who didn't always get a decent meal. Latifah had been raised in a Muslim home where her parents said daily prayers, kept dietary rules, and observed holidays. But once she left for college, she adopted the secular habits of her friends and now just thought of herself as Muslim without worrying about doing much. Petra's family was Greek Orthodox—but no one in her family had attended more than a baptism or wedding for years. They came to Grace because they enjoyed the cadre of young people and the opportunity to do something that made a difference.

Emily and Jon generally join the worshiping community while Petra, Latifah, and a loose group of young adults from the lunch crew regroup at the Starbucks café built into one corner of the church building. Emily, Jon, and others in the congregation often come into the café after the service and can usually find people from church floating in and out of the café during the afternoon. One table got dubbed "the altar" and the gang gathers around it, enjoying each other's company. It is not unusual to find that the conversation has turned to God and faith. While most in this group do not think of themselves as Christian, they have found a home at Grace Church. The chance to serve, the conversation at the café, and the late afternoon prayer service feels right to them. So they show up...and often bring friends. Some members of the church hang out with them and participate in the conversations, but there never is any pressure for them to "join"—which is a good thing because this gang has no intention of being church members!

It is a warm summer day and the café has tables out on the street. The usual group of young adults begins to gather as the afternoon wears on, and Emily finds herself spending the afternoon there, just hanging out. A bunch of them have just decided to check out a new club that night when the church bell begins to toll. "Ooops, prayer time," announces one of the young men, standing up. "Anyone coming?" One guy heads home to feed his cat and get changed for the evening but the rest of the gang enters the sanctuary through a glass door at the back of the café. "If you need a blessing today, my friends, feel free to join us for prayers," one guy calls out to the other café patrons. One woman looks quizzical so Emily stops at her table. "We have a short, simple prayer service that we do—it's open to anyone, any faith or no faith. Most of us aren't church folks but this is a real nice way to end the afternoon. If you want to come, I'll be glad to sit with you and show you what we do." "Ummm...well...okay," the woman replies. "I'm just starting a new job at Chase Hospital and moved down the street from here." "You'll love it here," Emily responds, opening the door to the sanctuary. "Lots of young people, great restaurants, cultural life."

The group is joined by a few others who wander in from the neighborhood. The service has been largely organized and led by men from the homeless shelter. They arrived a few minutes earlier and have arranged the chairs in two rows facing each other with a low table in between. On the table they set two icons, one facing each of the rows of seats, two bowls of incense that were now gently lofting swirls of smoke, and a bank of small votive candles. The lights have been adjusted to make reading possible but also to create a slightly dim and mysterious atmosphere. A small lectern flanked by two lighted torches has been set at one end of the opening between the two rows of chairs. One of the men takes his seat and unpacks his recorder, while another guy checks to make sure the readings are on the lectern. Emily and her new friend join those who are gathering, picking up a booklet with the service in it before taking their seats.

Silence descends as the man with the recorder begins to play a quietly haunting piece. The service is simple, and includes readings from the Bible and a book of poems. The group chants a psalm—Emily remembered her surprise the first time she read the instructions: "Pick a note, any note, and just sing/say the psalm on that note. Don't worry about the fact that everyone else will be chanting on a different note—it will be fine." And it was—in fact, it was beautiful. And fortunately it didn't require any musical skill. Even the guy who claimed he was a monotone singer fit right in. The woman who came with Emily joins in immediately. Later they sing a couple of Taizé chants—simple, repetitive songs accompanied by the recorder and led by one man who has a strong voice. Others pick up the tune the second or third time around.

Latifah loves this prayer service. It isn't Muslim but she feels comfortable in it. She often comes for the service, even if she didn't help with lunch that day, and sometimes drops in on weekdays if her work doesn't keep her in the office too late. And she joins the café group regularly, finding that the conversations are challenging her thinking about God. In fact, Jon just invited her to a series on world religions that will be starting at Grace Church this Tuesday night and she has decided to go. Jon said he thought she'd have something to offer the group from the perspective of a Muslim who had been born and raised in an Arabic country, but Latifah suspects she will learn as much or more than she can teach.

"Want to go the club with us?" Emily asks her new friend as the two of them head out after the service. "Ummm, sure," the woman replies. "Where are you going? . . ."

one year later . . .

It is Easter Eve and there is an air of excitement in the church. A group of parishioners arrived yesterday and have spent all night in retreat with the baptismal candidates. Emily, her friend Petra, one of the guys who hung around the café for the past couple of years, one of guys from the homeless shelter, a neighborhood teenager who wandered into church a couple of years ago, and an elderly couple who met each other at the lunch and plan to marry soon are among those being baptized. They and their mentors have been preparing for this moment for months. They were admitted as candidates about six months ago and have been meeting with their mentors and in small groups to study the scriptures and examine their life of faith. They have begun a committed life of following Jesus, have identified and started exercising their ministries, and have developed a personal rule of life that is spiritually sustaining. They are now ready to officially join the Christian community and publicly affirm their commitment to Christ.

Emily is aware that this is an important decision in her life. She has decided that being a Christian is more important than making lots of money—her original goal in life.

In fact, she gradually realized that she simply was not comfortable being in a job where she was selling people something they didn't want or need—and that was ultimately going to be harmful if not the cause of a life-threatening illness. She recently left her job and is now learning a new career at a company that upholds her new Christian principles.

Petra was surprised to find herself drawn to Christianity—but no more surprised than her parents were when she invited them to the service. Her father challenged her about the value of doing it and seemed a bit worried about its possible influence on her. But her grandmother, the only one in the family who still went to church, was happy. In fact, she was coming from Greece to attend the service. "I know she's not going to be Orthodox," she declared, "but I'm just glad she's going to be a Christian."

The entire Starbuck's café gang is arriving—after catching a cup of coffee on their way into the sanctuary. The guys from the homeless shelter are filtering in, along with families and others from the congregation and the neighborhood. Those unfamiliar with the church are welcomed by parishioners who carefully intersperse themselves between newcomers so they can help them through the service. The poster, announcements, and invitations have all alerted people to the fact that this is going to be a *long* service but people seem to be prepared. Parents with children have shown up with sleeping bags that are stowed until the time when they might be needed; many of the younger children have come in new pajamas purchased especially for the occasion.

The church is dark with just a faint hint of lighting to guide people. Most people gather around the doorway area where a huge caldron sits waiting for the new fire. At 10 p.m. the service begins. The fire is lit and the flame leaps upward, startling a few of the children. The paschal candle leads the people to the seats around the altar. The Vigil begins—the Creation story is told by families scattered around the church, with a parent relaying the events of a day and their child responding, "And God said it was good!" The children reenact the Exodus story with enthusiasm and everyone gets into the act providing sound effects for the dry bones story from Ezekiel. Songs are sung with a panoply of musical instruments and styles.

Finally, the moment everyone has been waiting for arrives. Children who dozed off are awakened and gather around a large rectangular tub that sits on a large rug in front of the altar. A fountain has been keeping the sound of water audible throughout the service and the plants and colorful fabric around the base of the font have made it a focal point. Those to be baptized and their mentors have slipped to the back edges of the room. Emily and her two mentors come forward first. Paul speaks: "It is with great joy that Jon and I present Emily Elizabeth Gibbons to receive the sacrament of baptism," he says, his voice choking with emotion. Jon adds: "We affirm that she has studied the scriptures and the faith, that she understands the importance of this commitment, and is ready to give her life to Christ."

Emily looks around the congregation. "My friends," she begins, "over two years ago I started coming to Grace Church to help Jon cook lunch, never imagining that I'd end up here!" She smiles as people chuckle. "I came wanting to help out because I thought it was a good thing to do and it made me feel good about myself. But you have shown me God's love and goodness—to me and to all of creation. And from you I have learned about how Christ's life, death, and resurrection has made all of us one with God and with the whole creation. I came to this city for a job that was going to make me rich—and it did give me lots of money. But it made me poor in other ways. Being in this community has led me to realize that I don't want to be selling stuff that makes people sick—I want to be part of helping make people whole, healthy, and alive. I want to be part of sharing Christ's love for me with others. And so I come tonight to affirm my faith as a Christian and to be baptized in Jesus' name. Thank you for being here and for walking with me on this journey, and thanks especially to Jon and Paul, who have answered a zillion questions and asked me questions that I needed to be asked. Thanks, guys."

One by one the other candidates are presented—except the elderly couple, who are presented together and come forward holding hands—and each tells his or her story. The homeless man talks about how he found Jesus in the gutter and was led to seek shelter in a church. The teenager talks about how her home isn't a good place to be and how she found refuge at the church and a family who took her in as one of their own. The café guy talks about how he found God in the quiet evening prayer service and was drawn to learn more about the faith—almost in spite of himself. The elderly couple tell of the love they found in each other and the community.

The congregation listens, laughs, cries, and murmurs encouragement throughout the presentation. Then everyone stands and joins in asking the questions in unison: "Do you turn to Jesus Christ and accept him as your Savior?" the community asks. "I do!" the candidates reply. The mentors then lead everyone through the Apostles' Creed and Baptismal Covenant, and the priest blesses the water. Then one by one the candidates step into the font and kneel in the water. "Emily Elizabeth, we baptize you in the name of the Father and of the Son and of the Holy Spirit," Jon and Paul say together as they jointly pour a large pitcher of water over her and the priest anoints her with oil. They then escort her out to a side room while the next mentor team baptizes their candidate.

When all the baptisms are finished, the priest invites members of the congregation to come forward and bless themselves with the baptismal water while everyone sings a song. When the song is finished there are a few seconds of silence and then a drum roll begins. The door to the side room opens and the baptismal candidates, now vested in white robes emerge, followed by their mentors. The drum is gradually joined by the children using cymbals and other hand instruments until, in a crescendo of sound, the candidates take their places around the altar. "We receive you into the household of God. Confess the faith of Christ crucified, proclaim his resurrection, and share with us in his eternal priesthood," the congregation almost shouts.

A teenager begins beating the Chinese gong at an increasing tempo and the children scamper to find bells as the baptismal candidates call out, "Alleluia! Christ is risen!" and the congregation roars back, "Christ is risen indeed! Alleluia!" The children begin ringing their bells like crazy, dancing around joyfully. The organ bursts into life and everyone joins in singing a wild, crazy, glorious song during which the entire place is transformed. Candles are lit and the lights turned up, flowers appear from hidden corners and are grouped around the altar and font. The baptismal candidates bring bread and wine to the altar and then invite the people to gather around. When all is ready, the song fades away and the homeless man, whom the baptismal candidates have chosen, steps in front of the altar and tells the story of Christ's resurrection with tears of joy running down his face. When he finishes, the community celebrates the Eucharist together, the baptismal candidates receiving the bread and wine and then standing around the altar to offer it to members of the congregation.

"Man, it's almost two o'clock in the morning!" exclaims one of the café guys after the service. "I had no idea we'd been here four hours!" He gives Emily a congratulatory hug. "Okay, lady," he says, "I got that this is a really big deal. But now you have to tell me all about it. I mean, this was something like I've never seen but I think you're onto something. And I want to know why you did this." "No problem," Emily replies. "When do you want to start?"

# A Guide for Discussion

You may of course read the books in this series on your own, but because they focus on the transformation of the Episcopal Church in the twenty-first century the books are especially useful as a basis for discussion and reflection within a congregation or community. The questions below are intended to generate fruitful discussion about the congregations with which members of the group are familiar.

Each group will identify its own needs and will be shaped by the interests of the participants and their comfort in sharing personal life stories. Discussion leaders will wish to focus on particular areas that address the concerns and goals of the group, using the questions and themes provided here simply as suggestions for a place to start the conversation.

# changing church, changing world

In this chapter Linda Grenz notes that "how the church makes and nurtures...disciples has changed over the centuries, in order to meet the needs of the people living in any given time" (p. 4).

+ What was your experience of Christian formation and education as a child? How was it helpful? How was it lacking?

+ What has been your experience of Christian formation and education as an adult? How has it helped you to grow in faith? What is missing for you?

+ What aspects of church life have nurtured your faith and encouraged you in ministry to others?

◆　◆　◆　◆　◆

Grenz emphasizes the need for "lifelong formation" in the church, especially in our multireligious, increasingly secular culture. In such a world she believes that the church "must be engaged in intensive, intentional Christian formation throughout the life of every Christian" (pp. 22–23).

+ How do the cultural experiences of your childhood continue to shape your religious beliefs and practices today? How have these experiences changed?

+ How has the church shaped your faith and life? How is the church helping to "form" your Christian identity and life today?

+ What could the church do that would help form you as a more faithful disciple of Christ in the next year?

# making disciples

In this chapter Grenz considers the implications of baptism, noting that "the restoration of the baptismal liturgy to Sunday morning and the focus on the Baptismal Covenant has probably done more than anything else to shape the Episcopal Church since 1979" (p. 25).

* In what ways has the 1979 Prayer Book's emphasis on baptism affected your understanding of yourself as a Christian, and your life in the church?

* Turn to the questions following the creed in the baptismal liturgy (BCP 304–305). How has each one shaped and informed your Christian faith and life? How might you live them more fully, more faithfully in the future? In what ways have they been experiences of transformation for you?

✦　✦　✦　✦　✦

Grenz believes that "if we want to move all of us from being consumers of religion to being full participants in the life of faith, we need to raise expectations and raise the vision of the promises of the faith" (p. 38).

* In what ways have you been a "consumer of religion" rather than a "full participant" in the Christian life? How has your congregation accepted—or even encouraged—members to be passive consumers of the church's ministries?

* What expectations for discipleship need to be raised in your congregation? Where do you see a fresh, renewed vision of what it means to be a Christian expressed in the church today?

### building blocks for transformation

In this chapter Grenz explores some of the best ideas and practices congregations are using today to build communities in which Christians are formed in discipleship.

✦ Discuss the ideas in the section "Laying the Foundation" (pp. 52–61) as they apply to your own congregation.
  – How are relationships developed and sustained?
  – Is learning considered important at all ages, or only for the young?
  – How are decisions made about educational choices?
  – In what ways is your congregation a "learning community"?

✦ Discuss the ideas in the section "Approaches to Learning" (pp. 61–71) as they apply to your own congregation.
  – Which of these approaches have you experienced in your congregation? Which ones are missing?
  – How does your congregation "educate the whole person"? What spiritual practices are encouraged and taught? Who participates?
  – What connections does your congregation make with Christians in other parts of the world?

✦ Discuss the ideas in the section "The Ministry of the Baptized" (pp. 71–76) as they apply to your own congregation.
  – What does "baptismal ministry" mean in your congregation? How do you see it practiced?
  – How would you re-envision the church as a community of people who are transformed by Christ?

In this chapter Grenz describes many of the resources currently available for Christian formation, and looks toward new resources needed for the church to be a place of transformation.

 ◆ Consider the educational and formational opportunities for children in your congregation.
    – What is working well? Why? What needs are not yet being addressed? How could they be met?
    – How are children learning to pray? How do they participate in worship? What are they learning about the Bible and the Christian tradition? How are their lives changed by what they learn in church?

 ◆ Consider the educational and formational opportunities for youth in your congregation.
    – What is working well? Why? What needs are not yet being addressed? How could they be met?
    – How are young people learning to pray? How do they participate in worship? What are they learning about the Bible and the Christian tradition? How are their lives changed by what they learn in church?

 ◆ Consider the educational and formational opportunities for adults, including young adults and older adults, in your congregation.
    – What is working well? Why? What needs are not yet being addressed? How could they be met?
    – How are you learning to pray and participate in worship? What are you learning about the Bible and the Christian tradition? How has your life been changed by what you learn in church?
    – What is keeping you from trying new resources that might bring fresh approaches to learning?

chapter five
### a new vision of discipleship

In this chapter Grenz tells the story of a congregation that has embraced many of the transformational practices she describes in earlier chapters.

- ♦ What are your impressions of this congregation? Would you like to worship there? Why or why not? Would you become a member?

- ♦ Identify some of the transformational practices Grenz has woven into this congregation's story. For example:
  - What is its theology of ministry?
  - Who are the teachers? the ministers? the members?
  - How are its faith traditions taught and practiced?
  - What principles inform and guide its worship?
  - How are young people formed in faith?
  - How are newcomers welcomed and incorporated?
  - What is the congregation's relationship with the wider community?

- ♦ If your congregation were to incorporate some of these transformational practices into its life and ministry, what would it look like? What would need to change?

# Resources

---

programs for children

CATECHESIS OF THE GOOD SHEPHERD

www.cgsusa.org

The website provides a catalog with several good resources about the program and includes materials in Spanish. *Catechesis of the Good Shepherd* is used in thirty-two different countries around the world so is available in lots of languages.

GODLY PLAY

www.godlyplay.org

The Center for the Theology of Childhood coordinates the training for *Godly Play;* www.godlyplay.com sells the wooden objects used in the program. The stories are in a set of books available through *Living the Good News,* an imprint of Church Publishing (www.churchpublishing.org). You can see a brief demonstration of the storytelling method on the *Godly Play* website and you can purchase videos with Berryman demonstrating the method with a couple of stories. A number of churches are identified at the website as "Centers of Excellence" and can be contacted to view their classroom.

## CHILDREN AT WORSHIP:
## CONGREGATIONS IN BLOOM
## www.childrenatworship.org

This grassroots organization developed by Caroline Fairless offers consultants who will work with congregations who wish to incorporate children into the life of the church more intentionally and fully. The website offers resources for worship, and members in the organization receive a quarterly newsletter and program planning catalog, and additional resources for leaders.

## THE WORKSHOP ROTATION MODEL™
## www.rotation.org

The website has lots of information, over three thousand free lesson plans, and ways to connect with others. The Workshop Rotation Model™ has shown that it is possible to develop and distribute resources on informal networks and through the internet with no connection to any denominational headquarters. It is a "movement" that embodies the concept of grassroots resources development.

*WorkshopCycles* is a Workshop Rotation Model™ curriculum by Tracey Herzer, an Episcopal educator, among others. It includes sacraments and seasons as well as Bible stories and concepts. You can download and try a free lesson set (a cycle), buy individual cycles, or get an annual membership. The advantage to the membership is that the cost is based on your average Sunday attendance and is very reasonable compared to other published curricula. *WorkshopCycles* is available from www.LeaderResources.org.

*Cornerstones* (www.cstones.com) and *The Potter's Workshop* (www.potters-workshops.com) grew out of the original Chicago Rotation movement and have both been around for a long time. They have many lessons available, though their prices can be prohibitive for some churches. Cornerstones has a great outline for how to get Workshop Rotation started in your church (www.cstones.com/workshop.htm).

Other denominational publishers also carry Workshop Rotation Model™ curricula:

* AugsburgFortress Press (Lutheran) has *Akaloo* (www.augsburgfortress.org);
* Cokesbury (Methodist) has *PowerXpress* (www.cokesbury.com);
* the Presbyterians have *We Believe Workshop* (www.pcusa.org/webelieve/workshop).

Most of these publishers provide print materials that look like traditional Sunday school materials (four-color with posters, handouts, craft projects, etc.) rather than the more "home-grown" feel of the grassroots versions. The cost of these materials is, consequently, higher. On the other hand, many of them offer additional resources (like music CDs) that make planning easier.

---

programs for youth

YOUTH MINISTRY AND SPIRITUALITY PROJECT
www.ymsp.org

The Youth Ministry and Spirituality Project integrates relational youth ministry and spirituality; in it the youth leader functions as a spiritual guide for young people. This contemplative approach to youth ministry has no "curriculum" (although Mark Yaconelli recommends J2A as very compatible and useful resource materials). A number of helpful articles, documents and resources are available at their website and they offer training for adults interested in using their approach. Yaconelli has also written several books about his experience in youth ministry, including *Contemplative Youth Ministry: Practicing the Presence of Jesus* and *Grow Souls: Experiments in Contemplative Youth Ministry.*

THE YOUTH AND FAMILY INSTITUTE
www.youthandfamilyinstitute.org

This program of the Evangelical Lutheran Church in America is a peer ministry program that uses the principles of relational youth ministry with a twist: the modeling comes from a relationship with a peer. They offer resources and training through their website at www.peerministry.org.

JOURNEY TO ADULTHOOD

www.LeaderResources.org

This program is a six-year process of spiritual formation that is available through an annual congregational or diocesan (judicatory) membership. You can download sample pages at the LeaderResources website. Local training workshops and a national three-day *J2A* institute are available for youth leaders and coordinators.

---

programs for adults of all ages

THE ALPHA COURSE

www.alphana.org

*The Alpha Course* is a ten-week basic introduction to the Christian faith. It seeks to answer the question: "Is there more to life than this?" It is built around a series of ten talks, weekly small group discussions (generally with dinner), and an optional weekend or day away to focus on the person and work of the Holy Spirit. *Alpha* began at Holy Trinity Brompton, an Evangelical Anglican congregation in London, but quickly spread throughout the world. The course attained its present form in 1992 and since then has spread to 154 countries and has been translated into 61 languages and Braille.

There is an *Alpha Course* for college and university students that recognizes that circumstances facing college students today require some creativity and flexibility, so it offers a manual with advice and ideas on how to tackle the issues facing college students today.

VIA MEDIA

www.everyvoice.net

*Via Media* is a similar program to *Alpha* but was developed by progressive Episcopalians in the United States and is designed to "proclaim the Good News of God in Christ Jesus and to present the Episcopal Church in a contemporary context." It has the benefit of being one of the few resources that is intentionally inclusive of people from a broad range of races and walks of life. It incorporates study, prayer, and conversation surrounded by radical hospitality.

*Via Media* is an eight-week course of study that addresses topics such as God the creator, Jesus, the Holy Spirit, the Bible, sin, the kingdom of God, and the Anglican tradition of a Christian home; it also explores the meaning and experience of baptism and Eucharist. It is designed for those new to church, people who are returning to the church after a time away, and people who are looking for an opportunity to explore their faith more deeply. The video presentations are followed by guided discussion, a meal, closing worship, and take-home materials for reflection during the week.

## EMMAUS: THE WAY OF FAITH

Course materials for the United States are available from Church Publishing (www.churchpublishing.org); the website for the United Kingdom gives more information about the program: www.e-maus.org.uk

*Emmaus* is a multiphase study program that is designed to welcome people into the Christian faith and the life of the church. It aims to involve the whole church in evangelism, the nurture of new believers, and ongoing Christian discipleship. *Emmaus* was developed by Evangelical Anglican clergy in England, and is modeled after the story of Jesus walking with two disciples on the road to Emmaus after his resurrection. The program is divided into three stages: *Contact, Nurture,* and *Growth,* to serve Christians who are at different points in their faith journey.

♦ *Contact* is a practical, hands-on resource that helps churches connect with those outside the church.

♦ *Nurture* is a fifteen-session course for seekers, new Christians, and adult confirmands. It offers five sessions on each of the following: what Christians believe, how Christians grow, and living the Christian life.

◆ *Growth* contains five short courses to encourage
believers toward maturity in key areas of the Christian
life: prayer; the scriptures; being church; worship; and
life, death, and Christian hope.

## THE KLESIS PROJECT

www.http://www.connect-course.org

The Klesis Project is made up of three courses—*Connect?,
Commit?* and *Covenant!*—meant to lead someone from
entering the Christian community to deeper life in faith.
*Klesis* is Greek for "calling;" the program thus explores God's
call to each person.

◆ *Connect?* is free of charge. It is designed to help participants decide if they want to deepen their relationship
with God through the local congregation. It is intended
for those outside the church, those on the fringe of the
church, and those who have attended for years. The
focus is on the Eucharist in order to help participants to
make sense of their experience of worship.

◆ *Commit?* is a twelve-week opportunity to participate in
a warm, supportive community exploring the big questions about who God is and what it might mean for you
personally to live more deeply into who you are in
Christ. The journey is structured around the Baptismal
Covenant.

◆ *Covenant!* is still under development, and follows the
two previous programs. It is designed for a group to
meet over at least six months to strengthen a sense of
God's particular call and to consider how each person
might develop a rhythm of life in response to that call.

## JOURNEY IN FAITH

www.LeaderResources.org

*Journey in Faith* is a multifaceted process of faith formation
that integrates Bible study, spirituality, leadership development, mission, and ministry. It is designed for groups of six
to twelve adults who want a more structured format for

learning and reflecting on their faith. The program is built around a Eucharist-based foundational statement: "We are a community, gathered and sent forth by the Spirit, to encounter our story, to be washed and renewed, to be fed, with thanksgiving, and to celebrate and serve the reign of God."

The groups are self-led with an optional "companion" as a mentor. They set their own schedule and progress through each "path" at their own speed. The paths, some of which are still under development, include the scriptures, theology, ethics, history, world religions, and mission. Each "path" has six units, each comprised of six steps (sessions) for a total of thirty-six core sessions in each path plus optional focus units.

*Journey in Faith* encourages participants to develop a rule of life including prayer, scripture reading, and disciplined reflection. Each unit introduces a new prayer method that is practiced in that unit and in daily prayer. Each unit also introduces a leadership skill that is practiced by the group members in leading the group sessions in that and subsequent units. The process encourages participants to examine their daily lives and apply what they learn to their day-to-day activities. The sessions start at an introductory level and gradually increase in depth and complexity. The process is designed to invite people into reflection and a deeper practice of their baptismal life and ministry.

### THE DISCOVERY SERIES: A CHRISTIAN JOURNEY
www.epicenter.org/edot/Discovery_Series.asp

This video series of programs is designed to help every Christian—new or lifelong, young or old—discover their own path to a life in Christ. Like our lives, careers, and relationships, our spiritual growth is also a journey. This series is intended to help everyone forge a lifelong relationship with God. Five courses provide comprehensive training for baptism, confirmation, spiritual gifts assessment, discipleship, and worship.

 • *The Path to Episcopal Worship* includes an instructed Eucharist, a history of the Episcopal Church, and information about the church's traditions and governance. It can be shown to newcomers, visitors, and lifelong Episcopalians to explain the symbolism in our worship and the polity of the church. (Three segments)

✦ *A Journey of Faith* includes basic information about the Bible, the Trinity, the kingdom of God, Jesus, the creeds, and baptism. The baptism segment may be used as a stand-alone piece. (Four segments)

✦ *A Path to Spiritual Maturity* includes an in-depth discussion about the importance of Bible study and different forms of prayer, both personal and corporate. (Four segments)

✦ *Our Spiritual Gifts* provides a guided tour of assessing spiritual gifts, defining ministers as "all of us," and instilling the importance of personal involvement in ministry, both in and beyond the congregation. (Two segments)

✦ *The Great Commission* shows how our stories are reflections of ancient stories in the Bible and teaches participants how to share their own stories with friends, neighbors, and coworkers, making disciples who make disciples. (Three segments)

## EDUCATION FOR MINISTRY
www.sewanee.edu/efm

*Education for Ministry* (commonly known as EfM) is part of the education extension program of the School of Theology of the University of the South. EfM is a four-year course of study that covers the Old and New Testaments, church history, and theology in a small group setting. It is college or graduate school level and requires an amount of reading that provides in-depth knowledge; it also hones participants' skills in theological reflection.

The seminar group of six to twelve participants and a trained mentor is the nucleus of the *Education for Ministry* program. The group meets weekly for the nine-month academic year, in addition to time spent in study preparation for each week. An important goal of EfM is to learn to think theologically and to develop skills in theological reflection. EfM groups are supported by prayer, and participants are encouraged to develop a pattern of worship appropriate to their situations.

## LIFECYCLES

### www.LeaderResources.org/LifeCycles

*LifeCycles* was developed by the dioceses of Northern Michigan, Vermont, Wyoming, and Nevada as a way to form and support local ministry teams; the initial developers have now been joined by the Episcopal Divinity School. *LifeCycles* is an integrated program of education and formation that includes the study of the scriptures, church history, ethics, and theology, and incorporates leadership skills and spirituality with a focus on the practice of ministry. *LifeCycles* groups have a companion but the sessions are led by the participants who practice specific leadership skills designed to be transferable to other settings. *LifeCycles* is designed to support its members in doing ministry and in changing the local church system to become a ministering community rather than a community gathered around a minister.

Over time, the development team became aware that the basic content sessions were valuable to all members of the congregation and not just those on ministry support teams, so they recast it as *Journey in Faith* (described above), with minor shifts to focus it primarily on ministry in daily life. The collaborative development process informs and infuses both curricula, which serve more as a guide for collaborative learning than a traditional "course of study."

---

### electronic media

## THE EPISCOPAL MEDIA CENTER

### www.episcopalmediacenter.org

The Episcopal Media Center was founded in 1945 as The Episcopal Radio and TV Foundation, and over the years has been instrumental in producing Emmy-winning television programming such as *The Lion, the Witch, and the Wardrobe* and *Shadowlands*. It has co-sponsored the Peabody Award-winning "The Protestant Hour," now known as "Day 1 Radio." The Episcopal Media Center offers audio books, videos, tapes, CDs, and DVDs. It can help congregations and dioceses use the center's television ads or to develop their own ads and strategy. More recently it has launched Alliance Technology Services, which provides churches and diocese with a variety of technology resources, including a unique integrated website template that includes electronic newsletter calendars, databases, file sharing, discussion groups, podcasts, webstreaming, blogs, email, event registration, and much more. The Episcopal Media Center continues to be an important resource in helping the church take advantage of technological advances.

LEADERRESOURCES
www.LeaderResources.org
LeaderResources offers over fifty programs for children, youth, and adults as downloadable electronic files that churches can edit and print themselves. An Episcopal publishing and consulting organization started in 1994, LeaderResources fostered grassroots resource development in the Episcopal Church by functioning as the "back office" support system for educators, congregations, and dioceses that want to offer their resources to the larger church. At the website you will find sample pages and a catalog that you can download, print and share with potential small group coordinators.

THE THOUGHTFUL CHRISTIAN
www.thethoughtfulchristian.com
The Thoughtful Christian is a website (similar to LeaderResources) by a Presbyterian publisher with downloadable weekly study guides that are designed to stimulate thoughts about Christian values and how they relate to today's world.

LIVING THE QUESTIONS
www.livingthequestions.com
> Living the Questions is another group that provides down-
> loadable print materials along with video presentation from
> a progressive ecumenical Christian perspective.

## publishers of curricula and books

CHURCH PUBLISHING
www.churchpublishing.org;  www.morehousepublishing;
www.livingthegoodnews.com
> Church Publishing now owns both Morehouse Publishing
> and *Living the Good News,* a popular church school
> curriculum for Episcopal, Lutheran, and Roman Catholic
> churches that is based on the texts of the *Revised Common
> Lectionary.* You will find a variety of adult programs and/or
> books at all three websites and can contact them to obtain
> catalogs that you can share with potential small group coor-
> dinators.

COWLEY PUBLICATIONS
www.rowmanlittlefield.com/Imprints/Cowley.shtml
> Formerly a press of the Society of St. John the Evangelist,
> Cowley Publications is now owned by Rowman and
> Littlefield. It carries a number of important books by
> Episcopal authors, many of which include study guides for
> discussion groups.

FORWARD MOVEMENT
www.forwardmovement.org
> This publishing house also publishes Episcopal authors and
> books that would be useful for adult education. It publishes
> a host of small pamphlets and booklets that are increasingly
> popular in a postmodern era where people are often hesitant
> to read a whole book. Creative uses of these small resources
> (put them in your church's bathrooms!) can be a highly
> effective way of reaching people.

AUGSBURGFORTRESS PRESS

www.augsburgfortress.org

    AugsburgFortress is the Lutheran publishing house, and offers a variety of books and curricula that are easily adapted to Episcopal congregations.

COKESBURY

www.cokesbury.com

    Cokesbury is the Methodist publisher, and also distributes books for Westminster John Knox, which is Presbyterian.

# Notes
# and Sources

notes

1. David E. Sumner, *The Episcopal Church's History, 1945–1985* (Wilton, Conn.: Morehouse Publishing, 1987), 74.

2. Sumner, *Episcopal Church's History,* 75.

3. *Time* (May 16, 1955); italics added.

4. Charles Price and Louis Weil, *Liturgy for Living,* The Church's Teaching Series (New York: Seabury Press, 1979), 102.

5. Pronounced *kat-a-KYU-men-ate.* Other related terms are: *catechumen (kat-a-KYU-men),* a person being formed in the faith and being prepared for baptism; *catechist (KAT-a-kist),* a person leading another person to full commitment to Christ; *catechesis (kat-a-KEE-sis),* a process for forming a person in the faith. For more information about the catechumenate today see the North American Association for the Catechumenate at www.catechumenate.org.

6. *Called to Teach and Learn: A Catechetical Vision and Guide for the Episcopal Church* (New York: Episcopal Church Center, 1994), 19.

7. From the Merriam-Webster dictionary: Middle English *obeien,* from Anglo-French *obeir,* from Latin *oboedire,* from *ob-* toward + *oedire* (akin to *audire,* to hear).

8. *Dynamic Learning Communities: An Alternative to Designed Instructional Systems* by Brent Wilson, University of Colorado at

Denver, and Martin Ryde, Storage Technology Corporation; http://carbon.cudenver.edu/~mryder/dlc.html.

9. The educator Edgar Dale developed this "cone of experience" in 1969.

10. See www.episcopalchurch.org/companion for more about companion diocese relationships.

11. Taken from Leslie Nipps, "An Anglican/Emerging Church Synthsis?" See the full article in *OPEN,* the free newsletter of Associated Parishes for Liturgy and Mission—a great organization to join if you are interested in exploring the relationship between formation and liturgy. http://www.associatedparishes.org/open/ Open_Fall_2007_Full_issue.pdf.

12. You can find out what is happening and download interim documents at http://www.episcopaleslatinos.org. Forward Movement is also launching a Spanish-language initiative. You can learn more about what they are developing at http://www.forwardmovement.org/ spanish.cfm.

13. See: www.godlyplay.org/view.php/page/research.

14. From the History section, at www.cgsusa.org/learnmore.php .

15. From the website www.childrenatworship.org. The manual *Children at Worship: Congregations in Bloom* was originally published by Church Publishing, and is now available from the author or as an e-book at www.LeaderResources.org.

16. This history of the Workshop Rotation Model[TM] is by Neil McQueen and is from www.rotation.org.

17. *The Seed of God/La Semilla de Dio* is available from The Center for Children and Theology in Washington, D.C.; www.cctheo.org/ SeedPressrelease.html.

18. Article at www.youthspecialties.com/articles/topics/spiritual_life/ welcome.php.

19. From the Youth Ministry and Spirituality Project website, www.ymsp.org/welcome.html.

20. The following description is adapted from the overview of *J2A* by Amanda Millay Hughes available at www.LeaderResources.org.

21. From www.peerministry.org/adult_training/about/barbara.php.

22. From a PowerPoint presentation available at www.peerministry.org.

23. Verna J. Dozier, *The Dream of God: A Call to Return* (Cambridge, Mass.: Cowley Publications, 1991), 142.

24. From website of St. George's Episcopal Church, York Harbor, Maine: www.stgeorgesyorkharbor.org/U2%20Eucharists/ u2charists.html. For information on ONE, see www.one.org.

25. Elizabeth Keaton, in an email to the House of Bishops and Deputies listserve, October 6, 2007. Used with permission.

Diana Butler Bass, *Christianity for the Rest of Us* (San Francisco: HarperSanFrancisco, 2006), 229.

Jerome W. Berryman, *Playful Orthodoxy: Reconnecting Religion and Creativity by Education;* www.godlyplay.org .

*Called to Teach and Learn: A Catechetical Vision and Guide for the Episcopal Church* (New York: Episcopal Church Center, 1994), 12, 21.

Sofia Cavalletti, quoted at www.cgsusa.org/learnmore.php.

Jim Kitchens, *The Postmodern Parish* (Herndon, Va.: Alban Institute, 2003), 28, 44, 61.

Anthony B. Robinson, *Transforming Congregational Culture* (Grand Rapids: Eerdmans, 2003), 31, 58, 61, 77, 103.

Linda Skaggs, First Presbyterian Church, Highland, Indiana, as quoted www.cstoes.com/testimonials.htm.